Bible Interpretations

Nineteenth Series

January 5 – March 29, 1896

Luke

Bible Interpretations

Nineteenth Series

Luke

These Bible Interpretations were published in the Inter-Ocean Newspaper in Chicago, Illinois during the late eighteen nineties.

By

Emma Curtis Hopkins

President of the Emma Curtis Hopkins Theological Seminary at Chicago, Illinois

WISEWOMAN PRESS

Bible Interpretations: ***Nineteenth Series***

By Emma Curtis Hopkins

Managing Editor: Michael Terranova

ISBN: 978-0945385-70-7

WiseWoman Press

Vancouver, WA 98665

www.wisewomanpress.com

www.emmacurtishopkins.com

CONTENTS

Foreword by Rev. Natalie R. Jean ix
Introduction by Rev. Michael Terranova xi
I. Missing 1
II. Missing 3
III. Lesson On Repentance 5
Luke 3:15-22
IV. "The Early Ministry Of Jesus" 17
Luke 4:22
V. Missing 27
VI. Missing 29
VII. The Secret Note 31
Luke 6:41-49
VIII. Answered Prayer 41
Luke 8:43-55
IX. Letting Go The Old Self 51
Luke 9:18-27
X. "Me, Imperturbed" 63
Luke 10:25-37
XI. Lord's Prayer 73
Luke 11:1-13
XII. "Be Not Drunk With Wine." 83
Luke 12:37-46
XIII. The Winds Of Living Light 93
Luke 12:8
List of Bible Interpretation Series 104

Editors Note

All lessons starting with the Seventh Series of Bible Interpretations will be Sunday postings from the Inter-Ocean Newspaper in Chicago, Illinois. Many of the lessons in the following series were retrieved from the International New Thought Association Archives, in Mesa, Arizona by, Rev Joanna Rogers. Many others were retrieved from libraries in Chicago, and the Library of Congress, by Rev. Natalie Jean.

All the lessons follow the Sunday School Lesson Plan published in "Peloubet's International Sunday School Lessons". The passages to be studied are selected by an International Committee of traditional Bible Scholars.

Some of the Emma's lessons don't have a title. In these cases the heading will say "Comments and Explanations of the Golden Text," followed by the Bible passages to be studied.

Foreword

By Rev. Natalie R. Jean

I have read many teachings by Emma Curtis Hopkins, but the teachings that touch the very essence of my soul are her Bible Interpretations. There are many books written on the teachings of the Bible, but none can touch the surface of the true messages more than these Bible interpretations. With each word you can feel and see how Spirit spoke through Emma. The mystical interpretations take you on a wonderful journey to Self Realization.

Each passage opens your consciousness to a new awareness of the realities of life. The illusions of life seem to disappear through each interpretation. Emma teaches that we are the key that unlocks the doorway to the light that shines within. She incorporates ideals of other religions into her teachings, in order to understand the commonalities, so that there is a complete understanding of our Oneness. Emma opens our eyes and mind to a better today and exciting future.

Emma Curtis Hopkins, one of the Founders of New Thought teaches us to love ourselves, to speak our Truth, and to focus on our Good. My life has moved in wonderful directions because of her teachings. I know the only thing that can move me in this world is God. May these interpretations guide you to a similar path and may you truly remember that "There Is Good For You and You Ought to Have It."

Introduction

Emma Curtis Hopkins was born in 1849 in Killingsly, Connecticut. She passed on April 8, 1925. Mrs. Hopkins had a marvelous education and could read many of the worlds classical texts in their original language. During her extensive studies she was always able to discover the Universal Truths in each of the world's sacred traditions. She quotes from many of these teachings in her writings. As she was a very private person, we know little about her personal life. What we do know has been gleaned from other people or from the archived writings we have been able to discover.

Emma Curtis Hopkins was one of the greatest influences on the New Thought movement in the United States. She taught over 50,000 people the Universal Truth of knowing "God is All there is." She taught many of founders of early New Thought, and in turn these individuals expanded the influence of her teachings. All of her writings encourage the student to enter into a personal relationship with God. She presses us to deny anything except the Truth of this spiritual Presence in every area of our lives. This is the central focus of all her teachings.

The first six series of Bible Interpretations were presented at her seminary in Chicago, Illinois. The remaining Series', probably close to thirty, were printed in the Inter Ocean Newspaper in Chicago. Many of the lessons are no longer available for various reasons. It is the intention of WiseWoman Press to publish as many of these Bible Interpretations as possible. Our hope is that any missing lessons will be found or directed to us.

I am very honored to join the long line of people that have been involved in publishing Emma Curtis Hopkins's Bible Interpretations. Some confusion exists as to the numbering sequence of the lessons. In the early 1920's many of the lessons were published by the Highwatch Fellowship. Inadvertently the first two lessons were omitted from the numbering system. Rev. Joanna Rogers has corrected this mistake by finding the first two lessons and restoring them to their rightful place in the order. Rev. Rogers has been able to find many of the missing lessons at the International New Thought Alliance archives in Mesa, Arizona. Rev. Rogers painstakingly scoured the archives for the missing lessons as well as for Mrs. Hopkins other works. She has published much of what was discovered. WiseWoman Press is now publishing the correctly numbered series of the Bible Interpretations.

In the early 1940's, there was a resurgence of interest in Emma's works. At that time, Highwatch Fellowship began to publish many of her writings, and it was then that *High Mysticism*, her seminal work was published. Previously, the material contained in High Mysticism was only available as individual lessons and was brought together in book form for the first time. Although there were many errors in these first publications and many Bible verses were incorrectly quoted, I am happy to announce that WiseWoman Press is now publishing *High Mysticism* in the a corrected format. This corrected form was scanned faithfully from the original, individual lessons.

The next person to publish some of the Bible Lessons was Rev. Marge Flotron from the Ministry of Truth International in Chicago, Illinois. She published the Bible Lessons as well as many of Emma's other works. By her initiative, Emma's writings were brought to a larger audience when DeVorss & Company, a longtime publisher of Truth Teachings, took on the publication of her key works.

In addition, Dr. Carmelita Trowbridge, founding minister of The Sanctuary of Truth in Alhambra, California, inspired her assistant minister, Rev. Shirley Lawrence, to publish many of Emma's works, including the first three series of Bible Interpretations. Rev. Lawrence created mail order courses for many of these Series. She has graciously passed on any information she had, in order to assure that these works continue to inspire individuals and groups who are called to further study of the teachings of Mrs. Hopkins.

Finally, a very special acknowledgement goes to Rev Natalie Jean, who has worked diligently to retrieve several of Emma's lessons from the Library of Congress, as well as libraries in Chicago. Rev. Jean hand-typed many of the lessons she found on microfilm. Much of what she found is on her website, www.highwatch.net.

It is with a grateful heart that I am able to pass on these wonderful teachings. I have been studying dear Emma's works for fifteen years. I was introduced to her writings by my mentor and teacher, Rev. Marcia Sutton. I have been overjoyed with the results of delving deeply into these Truth Teachings.

In 2004, I wrote a Sacred Covenant entitled "Resurrecting Emma," and created a website, www.emmacurtishopkins.com. The result of creating this covenant and website has brought many of Emma's works into my hands and has deepened my faith in God. As a result of my love for these works, I was led to become a member of WiseWoman Press and to publish these wonderful teachings. God is Good.

My understanding of Truth from these divinely inspired teachings keeps bringing great Joy, Freedom, and Peace to my life.

Dear reader; It is with an open heart that I offer these works to you, and I know they will touch you as they have touched me. Together we are living in the Truth that God is truly present, and living for and through each of us.

The greatest Truth Emma presented to us is "My Good is my God, Omnipresent, Omnipotent and Omniscient."

Rev. Michael Terranova
WiseWoman Press
Vancouver, Washington, 2010

LESSON I

Missing

Emma Curtis Hopkins was absent on a voyage to Vera Cruz, Mexico to bring her ill son back to the USA. She left December 28, 1895 and returned February 6, 1896. This would account for missing lessons in this quarter. She may have mailed the two in January or they may have been written previously.

LESSON II

Missing

LESSON III

Lesson On Repentance

Luke 3:15-22

For who can breake the chains of forged destine
That firme is tyde to Jove's eternal throne?
"The Knight's Tale" — Chaucer
"Yo hoga, so hoga." — Moslem

On two days it steads not to run from thy grave –
    The appointed and the unappointed day.
On the first, neither balm nor physicians can save,
    Nor thee on the second the universe alay.

The golden text of today's lesson is: "Behold the Lamb of God, which taketh away the sins of the world."

The trend of the testimony is the doctrine of fate as a heavenly fact in the sense that since in heaven all that which ought to be is already accomplished, it follows of necessity that, as fast as the heavenly fact is visible, it will be seen as inevitable.

"Lamb" means neutral to everything on this earth, then "Lamb" means one whose gaze is on the heaven in our midst. His quality is inevitably a dissolver. He has got to dissolve everything that looks like matter, whether it is good or bad, and make manifest the kingdom which is of the third substance, neither matter nor spirit, neither good nor bad, neither male nor female, neither rich nor poor.

In his presence we soon discover "the chaine that firme is tyde" from "Jove's eternal throne" to our own necks, and when we are slashed across oceans and lassoed through deserts we like the process. To us it is nothing — nothing at all. The "chain tyde to Jove's eternal throne" is our theme.

Now, repeating the name "Jesus Christ" over and over, even without presuming to contaminate it by our explanations of it, does indeed hasten human destiny. But when any approach to "beholding the Lamb" is practiced by us we are hurried from pillar to post, from mountain to sea, from event to event, with breathless speed, but never a mishap overrides us, never a misfortune submerges us, never a good event gives us pleasure. We find that we are greater than our life.

Lessons on that of us which is greater than all that can happen to us have been going along in the Bible sections chosen by the International Synod for many weeks past. And even this very first lesson in the science enunciated by Jesus of Nazareth on the subject of having a repenting attitude forever has been up again and again. Repenting is "looking unto Jesus, the author and finisher of our faith," Jesus is the "Lamb" because he repented. That is, instead of watching the apparent motions of the heavenly bodies, he watched the real motions thereof. All who have studied astronomy will remember about the apparent motions and the real motions of heavenly constellations.

Lesson of Kindness to All Creatures

Everything has its real and its apparent motion. Holland wrote: "Life evermore is fed by death," but that is only an apparent motion. Life is fed from the "life fountain that springs eternal." This is the real motion. Men seem to profit by pushing their neighbors to the wall, but this is only apparent motion. Men really profit by doing the kindest and noblest they can conceive by even the squirrels that hop from limb to limb in the trees.

It was the apparent motion of success in the time of Jesus, as it is now, that to form a company and break up our neighbors in store-keeping and manufacturing would be to our honor, but he took the heavenly principle of doing unto others as we would that they should do unto us, as the actual way of maneuvering, man with man, to bring success.

He took the strange position that to seem to lose a battle by not fighting to gain it is the greatest evidence of gaining it; that nothing gained by fighting for it is ever gained. "My kingdom is not of this world. If it were, then would my servants fight?" Not even the freedom of the slaves by killing men to win their freedom is actual victory for freedom. No life kept going by fighting and struggling to keep it going is life worth living. Only the life that is the free, unwon gift of the eternal “lamb” is life worth having. This is not the dogma of civilization, but it is the dogma of Jesus Christ, who never fought for the good nor interfered with evil.

John the Baptist said he understood perfectly that there was a way of talking to men by saying that the divinity in man is all there is of man, but he had been called to the mission of showing men that all outward disease and misfortunes are caused by wrong thoughts and all good conditions are caused by right thoughts. He said that he really knew that thoughts are as hard to chase up and change as carbuncles and fevers, but his science of thought was the best way to call the world's attention to causes more subtle than the clashes of matter.

He believed in steps and evolutions, but he knew that there was a science more stupendous than steps and grades. He felt the evil of the world so keenly, and was so happy in good luck and good friends, that he was buffeted like a shuttlecock from gladness to sorrow and from sorrow to gladness every day.

Hence, the highest he could ever get in independent speech, was, "Behold" — look — to the man that is greater than good luck and great name, and stronger than the darkest misfortune. Behold the Lamb that is most glorious when most un-friended, most powerful when least aided, and what might be called most superbly defeated.

Defeat More to be Desired Than Victory

There are few cases in the world's history where defeat has been the greatness of a man. Wellington is only mentioned in foot notes, while Napoleon is heralded from zone to zone. Sir John Franklin's failure after failure made him famous. The defeat of the Spartans has blazoned them on the pages of history. Jesus was apparently so beaten even his most sanguine friends felt the shame of his low estate.

Whoever knows that the divinity that constitutes his actual substance is the only nature in himself to take notice of, soon stops being successful by fighting for it or trying to accomplish anything. What comes to him comes miraculously and no other way. What he tries to do he cannot do. What he wants he won't get. What happens to him is marvelous, but he cannot be happy in it, for it is not identified with happiness. What happens belongs to the third realm of his being, whose long untuned strings are more wonderful than happiness.

If a man, woman, or child is unwilling to leave happiness and misery forever let them not watch the divine in themselves, or know anything about it, for this is repentance, which has mighty works in its footsteps. Let them not name the name of Jesus Christ for that name has swiftness in its tracks. It strikes like dynamite against happiness. It crushes like The Car of Juggernaut over sorrow. It establishes a new order of things.

The man Jesus ran the risk. He let his bridges be burned behind him. He refused the assistance of legions of angels in over-powering Pilate and Caesar. He declined the vinegar and myrrh opiates offered by the wealthy Roman matrons. He took the same heavenly chloroform he had seen the sparrows breathe when stoned by boys, and the helpless calves swallow when gashed by men. He cast in his lot with the helpless.

He went fellowship with those for whose peace there was no voice lifted. So what he says of heaven is true. For his bruised feet walked on its golden streets as unaware of their bruises as the sparrows watched by the heavenly Lord. When he saw the sparrows falling he watched the divine chloroform they breathed. This was beholding the neutral to pain.

How could he help becoming himself an eternal neutral to pain — an unfailing chloroform to misery if he never beheld anything but chloroform to pain? How could he help becoming an indescribable neutral to happiness if he saw the eternal throne back of happiness, too majestic to be happy?

John could get no farther than to say: "Behold the neutral." By this unexplained command he aped himself fast from human experiences through the chloroformed glory of decapitation, an apparently unsuccessful demonstration of the effect of watching the Lamb.

He turned to watch the wondrous throne of Jove, to which his neck was chained, and found it very near. He could no longer preach the power of life over death or of goodness over wickedness.

Sin is Nothing but Partiality

This is what the story of John the Baptist means, the swift march of man from the teeth of happiness today and grief tomorrow. There was no pain in his decapitation. For the same breath that eases the sparrows wafted its mystery through his frame. There was no rejoicing in his human honors, for the unexplainable glory of majesty in defeat caught his heart's highest leaps and kissed away ecstasy.

It is a sin to be happy. The Lamb of God taketh away that sin. It is a sin to be unhappy. The Lamb of God taketh away that sin. Let it be understood that sin is partiality; nothing else; the tip of the scales to right or left. "Give me neither poverty nor riches," cried the ancient prayist. The third presence in this universe is Jesus Christ, without male or female partialities, without happiness or misery.

Ecce home (Behold the Man.) He hurried John the Baptist from partiality for goodness into the impartial state by his simply accosting him by the mysterious title, "Lamb." Read Luke 3:15-22. He made no attempt to explain the title. He only told its awful mission with his whole gaze fixed upon the one man of all the world who was absolutely impartial. This cut off his own partialities.

Notice how in verse 16 he said that the mighty one was just behind him coming after him. So, in all ages Jove's eternal throne has been spoken of as just behind us all — just behind. Ruth, the emblem of the beautiful throne, said: "Entreat me not to leave thee, nor to return from following after thee." The priestly prophet promises. "Thou shalt hear a voice behind thee." The Holy Ghost descended from heaven upon Jesus, and his ears heard the voice. (Verse 22) This was the seal of his identification with the peaceable chloroform that wafts its compassionating ethers through all the maimed and hurt animals of creation.

The dove is not a fighter. Jesus never fought. The lamb is not a striver. Jesus never strove. The lamb and the dove labor not. Jesus never labored. "My father that dwelleth in me doeth the works." The dove and the lamb have no will. Jesus said, "I came not to do mine own will."

He identified himself with peace. So to look to the Lamb on Jove's eternal throne is peace. No pain to John. No pain to me. No pain to you. No pain to the creatures over whose uplifted cries we breathe the neutral winds of heaven.

Whatever principle a man identifies himself with he is bound to get its ways and means. He who is identified with peace cannot know pain. He who is identified with majesty cannot touch disgrace. He who beholds the fiery throne of Jove in its changeless splendor just behind finds that he has finished his course.

He may not attempt to help its wondrous footsteps. He may not think to be responsible for its glorious goings. "Yo,hoga so hoga." What is to be will be whether he sleeps on a pillow or rows up stream in a ferry boat? On hastes destiny. Fast rushes fulfillment of the promises which have always been told about the Lamb on Jove's eternal throne.

For the Lamb shall lead them and feed them.

When the man who sees not those mysterious interpretations explains these texts he talks very differently. Peloubet's notes on unloosing the latchet of the shoes of the Lamb read, page 23. "Latchet: The lace or thong by which sandals were fastened." Of whose shoes. As stockings were not worn, the feet would become soiled; and when persons entered a house the sandals were taken off and laid aside, so that the feet might be washed.

<u>God's Will Must Be Done</u>

On this same subject there are spiritual interpretations in imitation of Swedenborg much in vogue now among the Christian Science or metaphysical people. By these we are told that "latchet" is a loosing idea. One that sets the mind.... (line missing)....Shoes are protecting principles. Ideas with illumination in them."

One interpretation is for the right hand — the sheep; one for the left — the goats. They are prejudiced; one in favor of matter, one in favor of mind. But on the throne in the midst is the Lamb. Neither rendering is decapitating, hurrying, miracle working, marvelous un-explainable, unspeakable. The fire is on the throne science that notices neither of them. Nineteen hundred years of the Peloubet book style; one hundred years of the Swedenborg style. One year of the John the Baptist cry, "Behold the Lamb." John was put into prison by Herod March, A.D. 28, and decapitated March, A.D. 29. Let utterly free from the teeth of happiness on the sheep side and misery on the goat side by one year's recognition of the Lamb.

What God joineth thee to doing thou shalt do and no man can sunder thee from bringing to pass though he have thee in prison and scorneth thee and speaketh against thee, turning thy friends into foes and thy fortunes into wastes.

What God joineth thee to doing thou shalt do, though thou make a blunder and get an enemy at every turn of thy tongue. What God joineth thee to being called, that thou shalt be called though thy name is this moment a by-word and a hissing. What God joineth thee to owning that thou shalt own, though thou art poorer than the crippled pauper without eyes in the state poorhouse. For providence hath her house builded eternally ready for thee and beholding the Lamb shall reveal its unspeakable readiness.

There has never been a story of the throne of Jove so unimpeachable as this story of John concerning Jesus, the peaceable, compassionate man, all alive through eternity with God, our God. Wonderful John! Swiftly pulled from partiality for goodness through a chopping block of hate of goodness up to that impartial throne, he had kept his faithful watch on for just one year! Glorious John the Baptist, going swiftly to show how fast are the pulleys that string man to Jove's throne in its untold stateliness!

Wonderful story-telling of one who never cried out because seeing the Lamb cut him suddenly off from both the living and the dead. Comforting story, told to stop our tears for the hurts of a world. He crying not because feeling the Lamb's compassionating ministry of peace shows that whate'er betide him that seeth the lamb there is no pain. The Father that watcheth the sparrow breathing heavenly chloroforms through their pangs, and pacifyeth the animals when man striketh them to hurt, speaketh with a voice that annulleth life and death, hurt and peace, saying, "Thou art my beloved." (Verse 22)

"What I have called thee that thou art."

Inter-Ocean Newspaper January ***19, 1896***

LESSON IV

"The Early Ministry Of Jesus"

Luke 4:22

The golden text of today's lesson is: "His word was with power." The subject of the day must be called; "The Early Ministry of Jesus." The miracle offered as a practical fact for humanity to accept is; "That man may return to the 'beauty' and strength and charm of his youth."

It is not probable that many people will believe in the possibility of such a miracle as the return of man back to his estate of beauty and strength and charm after he has once arrived at the miserable presentments called middle age and old age. But let it be distinctly understood that the Jesus Christ offer to humanity is all miracle, and this return back to first base is one of them.

Isaiah, a writer of ancient days, felt himself inspired out of the range of his experiences to declare that such a miracle might take place. David, also, in a super state of mind, proclaimed the same fact. Read David's one hundred and third psalm and Isaiah's fortieth chapter. One has to be a transcendentalist to believe in such things before he has seen them, and he has to fill his pitcher of life at the same fountain where Jesus of Nazareth drank, before he can see them.

But this new age just dawning, has a tremendous impetus toward transcendentalism, and the newer interpretations of the words of the mystic-hearted Jesus are awaking to life in a world the chord that vibrates to the miraculous. So the divine meaning of this day's texts will certainly find 2,000,000 people in the United States, out of a total population of 70,000,000, who will believe in it.

Nazareth is a term which represents old or middle age. Jesus represents eternal vitality; eternal beauty; eternal fire. Nobody can get away from his Jesus, any more than Naomi could get away from Ruth. That is, nobody can ever get away from his own immortality. Suns wax and wane in heavens which no human eyes have penetrated; stars and the beings who made histories of them in rocks are forgotten in ethers of endless, boundless spaces; but the immortal Jesus in man, and in universe, returns again and again to Nazareth. This step of immortality on the globe of human existence for the purpose of bringing new life is related in Luke 4:14-22.

This lesson teaches one of those glorified facts in existence which shine so brightly that neither the physical vision nor the mental vision of mankind can see them, as nobody can eye the sun after a lifetime spent in a dungeon.

Nazareth citizens arose in wrath to plunge Jesus headlong down a steep place to stop his mouth for preaching the cure of famine and leprosy by stretching a welcome hand to the "miracle way" of getting on with life. Read on, from the twenty-second verse, through the chapter to find this good illustration of the natural opposition of old age to reinstatement of vital elixirs.

Two Ways of Getting On in Life

The theme of this lesson is also the two ways of getting on in life. One, by the usual plan wherein somebody grubbed and tubbed and toiled; And the other by direct ministration from the ever-full hand of the ever-present God, wherein we can see and know of no weary little children's labors, no stunted¬brained father's half-requited efforts. Notice how Jesus loved to tell them in Nazareth of Elijah's provisions for a starving widow because of her acceptance of the prophet, and of Naaman's wonderful cleansing through obedience to Elisha. So should Nazareth rise up like a young lion, and she that halted should become a strong nation, if she would let go her prejudices in favor of old customs.

"It is the custom to get decrepit," screeched Nazareth. "It is the custom for cats and dogs to quarrel," howled the cat in the fable. "It is the custom for somebody to drive bargains and grind the faces of the poor, that we may get our riches." urge the people. "There is no other way of wresting our living from the hard hand of fate except by hard work."

But Jesus Christ, the immortal spark of divinity, expressing itself, said:

"No."

They called him a carpenter's journeyman, but he called himself a king. They called him a peasant's offspring, but he said the absolute and eternal One was his father. They accused him of eating bread and wine to sustain his body with, but he said; "I have meat to eat that ye know not of." They accused him of working for his living at day's wages, but he said: "The words that I speak unto you, it is not I that speak, but the Father that dwelleth in me; he doeth the works."

This story of Jesus Christ, as expressing in bodily power the divinity in man, is the strongest representation that the world has ever had of what it can do and be.

There may some other man arise with a fuller demonstration about this time. Indeed, Jesus Christ, as dwelling in all men and also filling all space, said that he should return again and demonstrate one more point.

That point should be the close of the decay dispensation for all mankind. Nothing should fade or faint or fall. "I will see you again, and your joy no man taketh away."

When they chased him from Nazareth he was leaving an old custom to take its own run with humanity. But when this divinity chord presents itself plainly again, the Jesus Christ man will keep standing in his place and watching mankind in the face, till every knee bows and every tongue confesses that what he is every man is also.

<u>The Divinity of Christ's Ministry</u>

This time they watched him and heard him, knowing that he was asking them to accept his ministry as divine. They would not do it. Had the widow of Sidon analyzed Elijah as a common man born of woman, she would have starved with the rest of them. Had Naaman figured out just exactly what mathematical chances he stood for having his flesh return, fresh and young like a little child's, he would have held his leprosy, with the others. If Jesus meant to teach that there is no possible accounting for the direct interposition of the Divine afflatus with its feeding and curing by sudden miracles. It stands by itself, and wafts its winds through whomsoever it will, and whosoever accepts it un-questioningly knows no past and no future. He strikes the unalterable Real.

When Dr. Quimby taught what he called the Science of the Christ, declaring what the real facts of the case with man are, he showed how all misery is but an apparent motion of the heavenly man. By this recognition of the Real motion as contrary to and unlike the apparent motion, he took the sickness all out of people; the deafness, also, and the blindness. He set the captives free.

He taught them that by fixing the eyes on the motion and keeping them there, without analyzing the Real Man, but accepting him as a fact, any number of miracles would take place. So this day's lesson by Jesus offered most wonderful miracles, not only to Nazareth, but to the world. When poverty faces men it is an apparent motion of the heavenly body. Let man remember that and keep his eyes on it till it fairly dips him below the horizon of the possible and asks him to keep still for the impossible to happen.

This, the Nazarenes could not hold still and bear. And Jesus would not force them. There is one dip at the horizon point where it seems impossible to follow the offer of Jesus Christ. Rejection at this line of the seemingly impossible means going through another round of human experience no telling how many generations thereof. It has now been nearly 2,000 years since the Nazarenes fastened their eyes on the real motion of the heavenly body, and held still while the prophecies of renewal were being read, and while the eloquent preaching of book-writings was going on, but rose in disgusted rebellion when asked to accept renewal as their own in that very age.

Every pious man now believes in the marvelous as having once taken place, and in some future time to take place again: but he also declines to take for this day, this moment, the quick, manifestations of what in his mind he has always believed to be impossible. Especially does the old man hurl down the offer to have his feet set on the real track of life, where there is no decay, and no dealing with the world for his bed and board, and now the offer is softly coming up again, stealing like sunshine on the morning sky of one who has once preached boldly and read the prophecies in childlike innocence of earth's unbounded cruelty, but is now sitting down to see what earth will do with the message. (Verses 17 and 20)

There is No Power Save In Jesus

According to the prophecy, earth will accept it on this round. There has been a subtle alchemy going on through these years since Jesus stood in the synagogue at decrepit Nazareth in the sublime beauty of heavenly immortality, and offered to show the track of the actual man as the road upon which all men might walk. This talk at Nazareth has been filtering its mysterious meanings through the generations, even though nobody has preached it till the heart of the world is soft to the full sunshine of it as it rises, for the last time, to go no more down forever.

It is not necessary to preach this great meaning of Jesus, with its mighty stretches of power. He preached it thus once on the sandy brow of Nazareth, and now not a grain of dust blowing from Chicago to Sahara or from Sahara back again, but bears on its surface the impress of his face, all glorious with light, the music of his voice, all rhythmic with heaven. For, does it not say that his word was with power? And does anybody dare say there is any limit to the power of that word he preached? Has the continual insistence by our greatest preacher that he never meant any such thing as this reading tells, interfered with the subtle alchemy of his preaching that this renewal of youth like Naaman's and the provision from famine, like the widow's, were the actual privilege of all men in all ages by keeping the eyes on him and sitting still for him to do all the work? No. Their eloquent declarations have had no potency, for "His Word was with power." His Word had all the power.

There is no power except in Jesus Christ, strange as such a statement may sound. "All power is given unto me in heaven and in earth." This representative of the Divine chord running through the universe did represent indeed all power, but did not fulfill all demonstration till such a moment as all the world's heart is softened and chemically changed to hold still while the so-called impossible is taking place; while the customs of man throughout an earth's history are being nullified.

But that change has taken place. The secret doctrine has penetrated well. The people of the earth have touched the hidden ethers of that Divine presence, and the believers thereof are sufficiently powerful to make them ail keep still while the miracle of stepping from the apparent path of human life to the Real Path is taking place. "This is the acceptable year of the Lord."

Inter-Ocean Newspaper January 26, 1896

LESSON V

Missing

LESSON VI

Missing

LESSON VII

The Secret Note

Luke 6:41-49

Today's Bible Lesson has a mysterious way of repeating the one note in the Christian dispensation which the Christian pulpit never sounds. It calls attention to the secret vacuum around which all manifestations revolve. Does not the whirling, stormy sun sweep around a moveless axis? Does not the ocean cyclone lash and surge around a sleeping silence? So does all demonstrations of most powerful manhood and womanhood touch the wheels of efficient works by dipping the attention toward the silent note at the center of life.

And today's lesson turns the attention thitherward towards, and holds the attention there, that is towards the one un-preached note in the Christian dispensation. See Luke 6:41-49. That secret note had better not be named at the outset of this column of interpretations, because very few people would read the column if it were, for the reason that it is so unsounded within their own being that when struck they do not know that it is any part of themselves.

So we will let the note come out and ring its million golden bells on the ears of man at some unexpected turn in the paragraphs. First the golden text verse 46: "And why call ye me Lord; Lord, and do not the things which I say?"

This was illustrated very plainly to one recently walking through the factory of an American corporation, in Vera Cruz, Mexico. The factory is run by men who get down cm their knees and. cry; "Lord, Lord;" but the lifeless, hopeless faces of the little children working in that factory are plainly asking this question of the golden text. The corporation gives millions of dollars to charitable purposes and educational movements, but no fathers anywhere get pay enough for the factory toil of the kind those children are doing to loose the bonds of those little ones and send them singing hosannas in the highways.

But let it be distinctly understood that the Jesus Christ mill is run on that plan and no other. That is, on the plan of dividing up the gold and silver among the fathers so wisely that their children are free, and it is no use to suppose that a great monument or an iron box of government bonds can make a screen to hide the difference between the actual and the make-believe will.

If anybody should suppose to run a factory on the actual Jesus Chris plan, all those pious humbugs who run the wheels of trade and wages would laugh him to scorn.

It is well enough to grind down your neighbors and set your heels on their little children's necks, if you like to pattern your conduct of life on that fashion, but do not call it Christian. Call it Satan, just as it ought to be called, and honestly own up that you believe in Satan, father and patron saint of money getting, world without end, amen.

Secret Influence of Jesus of Nazareth

But this is not the secret center of the golden text and the whole Bible section. That center does not refer to conduct of life at all. It deals with something out of sight of conduct, yet which influence conduct. .

It is the cause of the golden text. It is that which makes the golden text possible. It is that which makes the other verses of today's lesson vital. Otherwise they would be s set of complaints against men for being naughty and praises of men for being good, which complaints and praises do not wash any better than tissue paper in practical life. For do not suppose that the men who underpays the children cares two Russian kopi about our description of his badness on paper or in pulpits, while beauty smiles upon him and club men feel it an honor to drink his wines? Of course not, and so we are only talking and writing "in our hate" as the saying runs, while we are moralizing at him.

Let us do Jesus of Nazareth the credit that believing he had some wonderful influence with which he was identified, that moved like an army with banner whenever he spoke and kept up its movement forever when set in action. “Heaven and earth shall pass away, but my words shall not pass away.”

He knew of a presence in this universe that operates on the most hidden springs of men and of angels. It operates through anybody who is consciously acquainted with it to as many as he deals with. This Jesus determined that he would be so perfectly acquainted with it that as many as touched him, whether by naming him or believing on his divinity; would feel an indescribable pull of their heartstrings afresh. To do this he found he must make himself as invisible to the flesh, as the influence itself, and he must call men’s attention to it by a violent exit out of their sight, as well a by preaching moral ethics.

Thus he made of himself a universal influence consciously drawing upon the life of the heart everywhere and forever.

“Wheresoe’er, in glory gliding
Shine the stars on nights of time,
There the wondrous magnet, hiding,
Draweth round it life divine.”

Whoever feels the pull of the divine strongly enough to live by it is as certain of the protection of it and instruction by it as he lives. Paul was much interested in this question. He said to the Romans that Israel would work and give and strive to be righteous, but would never get righteous because there is no such thing as finding out causes and effects by watching them. We must take the one perfect thing for granted and let it steer our ship of life its own way. "Whosoever doeth this shall not be ashamed."

Sympathy Not Always To Be Desired

So this is what Jesus was setting in motion by this sermon, which historians say he preached on the Horns of Hattin when he was 31 years of age the more we feel of the influence the keener our scent of his depth of meanings. It is pitiful to us to see Sunday school men and women trying to tell over and over, generation after generation, that good kind actions are more esteemed than riches, for it is no such thing. It is pitiful to hear them telling that our civilization is Christian victory, when it is all the product of grit, warfare, determined indifference to the rights of others, and hard work on the part of somebody or other, every item of it.

That which we feel strongly we «re sympathizing with, and increasing. We make it live as temperance women increase the drinking of alcohol. And as Christian Scientists increase poverty; temperance preachers by telling how great and powerful widespread rum is and Christian Scientists by telling that everything is nothing - nothing at all. One gets mixed into sympathy with galloping rum; and the other gets mixed into sympathy with galloping nothing.

The very first spring of Satan was sympathy with Eve. He felt so sorry for her ignorance. If you have neuralgia, and I feel sorry for you, feeling so tenderly for you that I know exactly how you .feel, I shall be the very one whose help you do not want. My sympathy doubles the pain and nothing I can possibly do with my hands or think with my thoughts will help you. I shall grovel down there in the slums of pain with you. This is Satan who shall crawl on his belly forever.

What must I do to help you? I must have compassion on you. What is that? It is giving you something that I AM in my freedom from pain. Freedom from pain knows nothing of pain. It is like the mother who nurses her hungry baby. Does she feel hungry? Does she cry with the baby? No. She is greater than that, she is absolutely indifferent to the hunger and the crying so easily does she fold the baby to her smiling bosom and comfort with the opposite of crying This is compassion. Nobody ever felt it, but was nourished beforehand to annul the troubles he met.

Two Ways To Choose From

This 41st verse declares that man must be nourished at the bosom of freedom before he has freedom to give. God is the Great Indifferent; the Smile; the Up-bearing, Nourishing Mother. Jesus fed at that breast and when the multitude cried with hunger He had compassion on them. That is, He had something to give them unlike their hunger. He was not a crawling sufferer with their sufferings. He had freedom to offer because he was free.

Here we touch the silent note of the lesson. It is the privilege of living by draughts from the Original and Changeless Mother God in our midst.

We have two ways offered us for being today clothed; fed, instructed. One gives us dust to eat, dust to fight, dust to mix with dust to complain of and dust to praise. We deal with the world according to the ways of the world. This is what we are doing when we hire little children's labor because it is cheaper and build hospitals for their bones broken in our service.

It is the dusty way. It is the same as having a fellow feeling for our poverty stricken brethren and weeping when their heads ache. All dust, said theLord to Satan, "Dust shall thou eat. Also he told him he would always stay in the dust as long as he existed.

The way of Jesus Christ is not dust. It is nourishment at the bosom of the Original of miracles. It is life and inspiration by the miracles by that for which there is no explanation. There is a law for working with dust for both mind and body: but there is no law for working by this free mother.

Paul called the great Smile from whose free ownership of the world the mighty Jesus drew his breath, "Sarah", He called the dusty mix of life with hiring out of my neighbors or as the grab name, places me over or under "Hagar". Jerusalem, which is the Smile God, clothing and feeding and instructing the Jesus Christ man by folding and providing and voicing in ways not believed in by dust, is free. She provided freely. Of her bounty there is no end. Read Galatians, 4th chapter. So how can I nourish you with freedom if I have not drawn from the free Mother? No matter whether it is from the naughty conduct I would set you free or from the hunger, or from the pain, or slavery. Notice how Jesus sounds, again and again, on this note of draughting from the Original for our wisdom, our beauty, our health, our riches. He repeats it over and over from the 41st to the end of the 45th verse.

Bring forth — bringing forth — bringing forth — not by the very best plans of dust. But by nourishment from the free Smile of the wonderful Mother we have called God. This is living by the miracle. Nobody shall ever know shame of hunger or neglect or forgetfulness who draws his good from the free Mother, and His Presence shall be compassion to mankind whose supplying name is now — not God, not Lord, not Love. (Verse 47)

"The Rock That Is Higher Than I"

For the name Lord make everybody who repeats it dictatorial and overbearing forever, supercilious also, and self-lauding. But this name will release others from the ever flowing fountain of power as Jesus did — Verse 47.

When Jesus of Nazareth changes the figure from fountain of freedom and trees of plenty, who to the everlasting rock of defense, by which the changeless and unfailing Mother will show herself to man; the sureness of the Mother is to her baby an everlasting rock. She is so different from the cries of her baby that she is as rock to waters. She is so much greater and wiser, so much stronger than her baby's smiling that she is as rock to sunshine and winds. "Lead me to the rock that is higher than I." Lead me to my Mother — God. Lead me to the rock under whose sheltering fastness I may be a rock of shelter for a world of victims to the dust man's breaths.

Who shall lead us to the rock? Not religion. She is the rock and the tool of dust: not Science. She is the analyzer of evil and good. She helps only the worthy poor on the dusty street of Chicago. And who are the worthy poor? Who calls them off in the court house and at the desks of dust? This Bible lesson says plainly that whosoever helpeth the worthy poor is poorer than the unworthiest ones he turns from his doors. The Jesus Christ man, nourished at the bosom of the Mighty Mother never asks who are worthy. "Come, whosoever will, let him come," he says exactly as she says. Over the raging waters, through the tropic miasmas, go take up your children, you who have been breathed on by the Infinite One. There is enough of bread, wine, meat, milk, shelter for youand all you can give unto. Enough and to spare. Moons may wax and wane, but the sheltering Mother God never waxeth nor waneth. She abideth forever the same, world without end.

As the white stars of the Southern Cross never change their faces, so Jesus Christ, from the cross of the eternal skies is yesterday, today and forever, the compassionate One in whose Name men and angels are safe forever. As the steadfast splendor of the four stars of the Southern Cross beams its mystic influences from some far regions which no man knoweth, so from the unexplainable heights of an unprecedented offer to men, Jesus Christ is that name of God which is synonymous of bounty, shelter, original Inspiration and swift journeying heavenward.

"In His Name shall the Gentiles trust."

*Inter-Ocean Newspaper February **16, 189***

Lesson VIII

Answered Prayer

Luke 8:43-55

Therefore will the Lord wait that he may be gracious unto you.
— Isaiah 30:18

"I speak and call Your soul unto its fate.
Tread bravely down life's evening slope,
Before the night comes do not grope,
Forever shines some small, sweet hope,
And God is not too late."
— Phelps

Today's lesson stands on the pages of illustrated sermons as declaring that nothing we have prayed for ever comes too late to fulfill exactly the mission we intended. Prayer is any method we take to address the Divine Presence.

Some people practice breathing inwardly deep breaths, and then outwardly, till there is a good vacuum within themselves. Ask them what they are doing and they will reply that they are getting God, who fills the airs. So they are praying. They accomplish really a great deal by this method of communicating with Divine Presence. We can see how far they etherealize themselves by studying up the present Brahman apostles and also the Buddhists whom so many Americans are now imitating.

Adam was not a conscious man till he breathed into his nostrils the common air and said it was full of God. He became a living soul the moment he appreciated that even common air is alive with sentience. Before that the words of Wordsworth were true of him.

"A primrose by a river's brim
A yellow primrose was to him,
And it was nothing more."

In other words, Adam is that state of any man while he is indifferent to the third substance that changes nature. And any form of exercise he may practice for the purpose of appropriating divinity is prayer which is bound to be successful.

Matter is one substance. It is not a quickening stuff. Mind is another substance. This is not a quickening stuff either. The third substance has no name. It is the quickening elixir which never fails, never changes, never moves. No man hath explained it though ages and ages of men have tried to explain it.

Some people practice words and thoughts arranged in systematic description of this third quickening substance. They have accomplished more practical works, perhaps, by their manner of praying than the breathers; for men do object to laboring with their breaths while they are fairly railing to labor with their thoughts and audible words. The healing practice inaugurated by Dr. P. P. Quimby of Maine about thirty years ago, and propagated by M. B. Eddy of Boston with her thousands of students, with which so much good has been exhibited as healthy bodies and so much self conceit has been fostered in all the minds practicing it, was all a thinking and wording set of descriptions of the third substance.

One Way Of Healing As Good As Another

The Italian physician who teaches breathing as a healing exercise says that he will not breathe even to get well by, unless he stands over them and insists upon prayer as well.

But the students of mind lingoing (specialized vocabulary of a particular field or discipline) work like cart horses all by themselves night and day, year after year, world without end, amen. They sometimes set up formulas of their own, and write articles explaining how superior are their new arrangements of the same old descriptions of Deity to the arrangements of their neighbors. This shows how well they love to work with their minds as a praying process for bringing something to pass.

Others beat the air, bend their bodies backward and forward, dance up and down like David and the Shakers of Lebanon, in an effort to get a touch of the third substance, with its quickening elixirs.

Today's lesson brings up these practitioners, and show that their way is as good as any. (Luke 8:43-55) It shows that perpetual practice of any one way acts like a force pump on the well of faith that lies deep down in all men's regions somewhere. And when that faith water begins to stream up, a man may use it to do with as he pleases.

It is a solvent to hard bunches. It is a washer out of misfortunes. It is a reviver of the dead, because it can strike down into the wells of water that even dead people never get rid of. It is an excellent thing to practice some operation with the design to lay hold of the quickening One, even if we get as conceited as Oriental adepts by it, for whatsoever object or purpose we direct our faith on is certain to be successful after a time.

This is declared by the patient activity of the woman mentioned in verses 43 to 48, inclusive. She had performed with money and instruments of various sorts for twelve years. She was always touching, reaching, exercising. Finally she hit it. The quest of her twelve years was ended. Her prayers by the hatha yoga system of physical movements was answered. Jesus Christ represented in his own form and quality the third quickening substance. So Luke declares. And touching him, she hit the very elixir she had been beating around after twelve years.

Never mind who derides your system; if you like it keep it, if by it you hope to taste the quickening elixir, for you are certain to get back from Adam to Jesus some happy instant. Adam is mind and body uncognizant of the elixir. Jesus is mind and body all alive with it.

The first practitioner hereby mentioned stands for American practices for getting hold of the third substance with its vitalizing energies. The second practitioner hereby mentioned stands for Asiatic practices for getting hold of the third substance with its vitalizing energies. Singularly enough they are both women. One is all worn out and hysterical with so much hard work, exactly like the religionists of America. The other is fresh and young, but still as death. She has no notion of wearing herself out, either in good works or good words. She represents the moveless religionists of Asia. Now this does not mean that some American religionists are not trying hard to keep still and be like the Asiatics, who can keep still as logs for six months at a time, while the birds building nests and hatching young on their heads never suspect them of being anything but dry sticks; nor that some Asiatics do not breathe and think and gesticulate for the purpose of getting hold of divinity, but that these are the main characteristics of

Eastern and Western praying strugglers after soul quickening.

Today The Harvest-Time

The beauty of this section of verses — 43 to 45 — shows in the assurance it gives that whether we wear ourselves to hysterics trying to get the main spring, or keep still as death for the same end, we are bound to get it.

If you or I have been discouraged because of the length of time we have been practicing our particular method, let us not be so any longer. For to let go of our method simply because we have performed at it a long time fruitlessly, is silly.

One arises and says: "Change now." This lesson says: "This is no time to change." Today is the harvest for both Oriental and Occidental, almost simultaneously. But America, harassed, hysterical, overworked, America first. Asia, still, inert, dead Asia, second. And these constitute the globe. Europe and Africa are merely flags thrown out to show from day to day how still Asia is getting on; or how hustling America is getting on.

Ministers talk for the hysterical one; verse 45. Ministers talk for the dead one; verse 49. So do they now. Some talk about activity as of no use. Some talk about stillness as of no use. The ministers are all flagging. But this flagging is only an evidence that the quickening spring is close. Jesus Christ stands for the quickening spring. We do not have to have a man with a seamless coat and sandals among us to convince us. The fact is sufficient. The final spring is now.

The divine light that blesses most through the verses of this day's selection from Luke is the tenderness of Jesus Christ, both with the nervous woman who represents American religious people, and also for the phlegmatic one who represents Asiatic religionists. It is most certain that both kinds need tenderness and gentleness from somewhere now

"The earth is fainting With long waiting For her living God to speak."

Over and over again it has been told in these lessons that the International committee was but acting as previously minded mile stones for the secret mechanics of this age when it selected the different sections for each Sunday to come. They were not aware and awake, but they acted well. Each lesson tells for the world and for each individual man and woman in the world.

"I Know That My Redeemer Liveth."

The touch of the right spring is at our finger tips. The sound of the right voice is in our house. This is so certain that there is no defeating their gentleness and beauty any longer. Years count for nothing with this presence at our side, with this voice in our ears. Though we are the threadbare with overwork, though we are dead with waiting to let the true one speak, we rise, we smile, we live again.

“For I know that my Redeemer liveth, and that he shall stand in the latter day upon the earth; and though after my skin, worms destroy this body, yet in my flesh shall I see God whom I shall see for myself, and mine eyes shall behold, and not another,”

This was the song of Job, who had faithfully practiced both kinds of praying, the active and the passive. And on the instant when it was most glorious for the sun of the eternal heaven to shine on Job, who shall say it was too late?

“Does the chrysanthemum not know her hour?” asks the poet. Some thing is near. We must not grope as against walls in nights without end. Some thing near calls. We must not make our ears thick with insisting that there is no life bringing One.

There is an end, a fate, a destiny, for every one. It is the lode star, the magnet, the quickening sun of each life. It is soul calling unto soul; deep calling unto deep, of which, if a man be aware, he shall sooner catch a hold than if he be unaware as this lesson plainly tells. But, whether aware or unaware the voiceless East and the tremulous West, at their devotions, have brought the age of seeking to its close.

What Job said represents both the East and the West. “Whom each one sees, and each eye beholds for himself, and no other,” man’s descriptions are any longer necessary. Though the years of man at his struggles have been countless, they now close up. And God has not come too late to me or to you, to Asia or to America.

Inter-Ocean Newspaper February 23, 1896

LESSON IX

Letting Go The Old Self

Luke 9:18-27

According to the deeper stream of interpretation of these international lessons the year 1895 was the year for the seeming triumph of the enemies of the generous and simple-hearted of creation, but the year 1896 is to show forth the actual ascendancy of these unsophisticated ones.

Today's golden text is one of the seals of this fact, though nobody can claim that it is an explanation thereof. The great facts of being have no explanation. Can anybody tell why one is one? Or why the circumference of a circle is a trifle over three times its diameter? Or why the angles of a triangle are two right angles? Neither tell I you by what eye-opening gleams the fact is as it is, namely, that there is triumph for baseness this year — even in a seeming prosperity,

To some people the science of mind is exceedingly fascinating, exactly as the science of stones is fascinating to others. To them it seems a clear explanation, a final resolution of the subject, if one divides mind into conscious and subconscious and explains that conscious thoughts, conscious words, etc., change the subconscious mind and make it show health of body, or disease of body; blue eyes or black ones; misfortunes or prosperities.

But to others the study of this performance is tedious and dissatisfying because they discover that it is only workable up to a certain point. They are always running up against an author, an original, a something which is independent of conscious and subconscious. At this point even a brainy discussion of the value of right suggestions to the gelatinous sub-consciousness seems childish and puerile.

The Nameless Something

How this nameless something that is independent of conscious and subconscious mind is what these lessons herein from Sunday to Sunday printed are always dealing with. There might be an allusion now and then to the pungency and governorship of words and thoughts in the daily life of a man interested in material things or mental things, but never let it be supposed for an instant that words and thought reach the daily life of anybody who is making this independent something his quest.

Let it be distinctly understood that there is a life to live, a set of conditions to have, vastly superior to any which our wisest thoughts can drub our conscious mentality into weaving forth for us. Under the splendor of this administration we discover that the solid muscles we build up by muscle-building thoughts are as liable to decay at the stumping place of conscious mind as the muscles we had in vigorous youth. Mind soon finds that the word life is no more useful to whip up the blood with than the word sawdust, after a spell of using it. What is the explanation of this? The same as that a horse does not read Sanskrit. This would be a wise and brilliant explanation to the world if given by students of the Greek and Hebrew words composing the Bible section under today's consideration. How can we tell this? Simply, because the willing millions upon millions of Sunday-school scholars are taught to regard exactly identical explanations as the height of spiritual wisdom, now attained unto by man on this planet.

Commening on Verse 20

Read the following explanation of the deepest signification of verse 20 of this lesson, as taught by an accepted commentary on the true meanings of scriptures "Christ is the Greek, and Messiah is the Hebrew for anointed. Anointing was the method by which Kings, and sometimes prophets, were set apart for their work."

This explanation of Peter's deepest meaning is satisfactory to the materially minded. It does not satisfy the metaphysically inclined. How do they explain it? They say that there is one idea in every mind which is ordained to purify and govern all the other ideas. They say that is Peter's meaning. But this is an explanation about as interesting as coal ashes to one whose attention has struck past matter, and its domineering thought toward the independent something which arranges life conditions by its own system, which no man hath seen at any time. "Neither tell I you by what authority I do these things," said Jesus. He was then married, united, identically one with that Author whom to know is to be; and who, if we only try to know, takes away our interest in conscious and subconscious mind.

The golden text of today is: "This is my loved Son, hear ye him." The verses selected to make us wise this week are: Luke 9:18-27. The mighty theme running through them is the unnamed something filling heaven and earth forever, whose dealings with man are direct if man looks directly at him; are indirect while being laid hold of by thoughts; are backward if handled in matter.

Men Move Backward

The evidence of the backwardness with which men dealing in matter lay hold of the Author of All is illustrated by their insistence that we must die to get into heaven. The evidence of the indirectness with which we arrive anywhere by thoughts is illustrated by the pauperism of the masses in juxtaposition to the adepts of Orient; also by the flinch of metaphysicians to the plan of doing without things in the days when the millionaires have boxed up the money of the world, instead of unclenching their fingers, or feeding the people around them. It is meant in these verses that the direct contact of the great Supplier with man shall be made. He who makes this direct contact feeds and provides for the masses without regard to the grab of the highway robbers of business. Jesus did that. "Go and do likewise," he said. It is meant by these verses that whoever makes direct connection with heaven shall have health and strength, life and wisdom, at once, as a bird has claws at once, when it touches the earth.

And mankind does not die to be fully equipped, nor does mankind have to go through any system of thinking with mind or laboring with hands in order to get this equipment. But the .thinkers and the workers are not to be scolded at. They like their way of doing things, and in due season they wake out of it as out of a healthy sleep. "Sleep on now, and take your unnecessary methods," said Jesus.

The 18th verse of today's lesson reads: "And it came to pass, as he was alone praying, his disciples were with him; and he asked them, saying, 'Whom say the people that I am?" Take notice that, though "his disciples were with him", Jesus of Nazareth was "alone praying." Nobody was ever companioned by anybody who asked him questions. Companionship is in mutual understanding and nowhere else. This holds as true in family life as anywhere. Jesus saw the disciples questioning who he was. He knew they had been discussing him with their Jerusalem, Bethlehem, Nain, neighbors. He knew it was better for them to be definite in what they had to say. As he had been praying to himself he had great respect unto himself. This self-respect was, on that day, to take root in others, also.

Importance of Self-Respect

Many, many days may man go on all unacknowledged, but if they never lose sight of their soul's noble exaction, and its majestic abilities, other men, also, will see it.

Self-respect first, then other men's respect. Home praying to himself. The father in him. "I and the Father are one." This is his third year of praying to himself as the Lord, the author, the head center of the universe. Evans, the metaphysician, wrote once, in a private letter, that it always takes mind about three years to recognize true power and show it out. How the span of self-recognition being about at its height in Jesus, the bold response of it in others was near. A man in New York sat one and one-half hours each day for a year and a half, for the purpose of making floating ideas in apace formulate themselves. He could not paint their filmy shapes on the darkened ethers with anything like success till after one and a half year's practice.

A certain woman shut herself to herself for three years to formulate the teachings she had received from the man who had cured her of some physical ailment. Many have sat with their minds focused on the healing spirit that runs so freely through this universe and have finally become healing winds wherever they went. But Jesus had the peculiar mission of recognizing himself as the authoritative center of creation.

He did this that others also might know their central majesty. What he could do for himself others also might do for themselves. He had voluntarily taken upon himself the same ignorance and foolishness that characterized them. "In his humiliation his judgment was taken away." He had the same one statement to cling to, and that one only, that they had. That was; "God is my Father." He clung to it on purpose. He tested it on purpose. With it for his unit he made a whole book of life. He had only got as far, where this lesson was talked over, as, "How tell who I am, ye people of earth?" The acknowledgement began then and is still going on. He has been all this time arriving on his own base steadily enough so that all people, all angels, all demons, also acknowledge that as Jesus Christ is God so everything is God. That as he strikes center, all strike center with him, for this center is identical with his. When he touches it indeed not only for himself but for them, they all vibrate. They jar. They totter. They fall, as to difference from their center, and expose their identical point of divinity with him,

The Companionship of Jesus

But while there is any question unanswered there is not conscious understanding, and therefore not companionship. The touch is not then made conscious to others than Jesus himself.

This lesson strikes for companionship. Jesus was preparing companions. At the very last lesson he gave that class he said, "Henceforth I call you not servants, but friends." While this lesson of today was going on he had no friends. It was the power of the Father to whom he prayed that gave him a hearing, even among those men. That power expressed was influencing them always according to the golden text; "This is my beloved son; hear him." It was that power he had been looking unto above which enabled them to leave Peter free to speak for them, all just what had stirred at their hearts' deepest strings.

"Thou art the Christ." This was not affirmation to bring out a fact, but simple expression of what he saw at that instant. His own light sprang forth, and by it he knew light. The light of Jesus penetrated him, and found his light easily. That man Jesus had the occultist's power of making other people do what he wanted them to, but he never used it. What there was of him he meant should spring from his own sight of his own center as nearly as he could strike it.

The healing power of the near future is to be the radiation of the quality we get from self-recognition, instead of the spread of our thoughts over the minds of others. It will be non-treatment instead of treatment. The more we let them alone the more divine their exhibition of health. What we know we ourselves are is their glory. This is shown by verse 21: "See thou tell no man." Let thyself know thyself. Let thyself be its own radiance. Think it not toward man. Speak it not toward man. What thou knowest on this subject is its own radiance.

Meaning of a Prophecy

In verse 22 he says: "The Son of Man must suffer many things, and be rejected of the elders and chief priests and scribes, and be slain, and be raised the third day." What was all this for? That nobody else forever need suffer anything, be rejected anywhere, die or rise from death. As all the grandeur of man should rise to bloom in his power, so all the misery of man should also rise to fullness in him. And the dispensation of regarding ourselves as trying to be at once with God should thus end. The dispensation of being hurt, either physically or mentally, should thus end. What should be the need of thoughts or efforts to get free from being hurt after that? If the mission of this acme of humanity did not close the dispensation of effort, to be at one with the Divinity on the throne of our own being, and close the dispensation of suffering for all who would not choose to stick to the old dispensation, whether it had any a existence or not, then he was a failure.

But he was prophesied to close the dispensation of death and pain by drawing them into his own body, and to close the dispensation of struggle to be companioned with God the Almighty by himself being companioned with the Almighty. And all death or pain, whether of mind or body, should thereafter be what we should be hugging as tatters of delusion.

"If any man will come after me, let him deny himself, and take up his cross daily and follow me." (V erse 23)

Of course it is something of a denial for us to give up our pains of body and our efforts to get rid of pains by some sort of treatment of them. Yet to let go of these rags because they have been worn once and destroyed forever is to be free. This was the mission of Jesus, then, to close the dispensation of suffering and struggle, both on the mind plane and the physical plane. This was the accomplishment of Jesus, then, that now man is everywhere free. He led captivity itself captive. Captivity starts in the mind. So by taking mind once he let us go free from mind. By taking body once he let us go free from body. And this is utter freedom, untrammeled being. Now, if anybody wants to save his mind and body, let him give them up in this fashion. Verse 24 teaches this.

It seems almost a shame to give up our mind on the offer of one man to take it, with its habits of harrowing us up to days and nights of toiling to arrive somewhere that nobody can get. But that was the vicarious business Jesus undertook and succeeded so well at that the wonderful demonstrations of new environments and new prospects, new characters and new natures are already begun for those who have accepted it, not by any efforts of their own, either mental or physical, but by the direct touch of something on the helm of their life working on different lines from their mental decrees. Verse 26 promises this. He cometh in his own glory and the Father's, and the holy miracles.

Jesus is Close to Men

Verse 27 teaches that sight of this accomplished mission of Jesus is simultaneous sight into that kingdom that does indeed lie close to our faces and under our feet this very moment. These interpretations, as they now run in this fashion, are criticized because they so often tell of this here present land, with its wonderful mansions, and of this wonderful offer of Jesus, the acme of philanthropic man. But they are what the lessons teach. They are what the prophets promised, the seers forsaw, the ancient poets loved.

"There is a kingdom on the earth, though not of it." "And with his stripes we are healed." "The chastisement of our peace was upon him." "He is the beloved son, hear him." There is a life to live quite free from thoughts. There is a life to live quite free from bodily needs and supplies. There is a life to live quite free from bodily pain, quite free from, bodily pleasure, as physical body counts; yet in that life nobody is foolish, nobody is a ghost, or wraith, or floating shape or mist in space.

In that life the mind of Jesus Christ is all the mind there is, and the body of that same one is all the body there is. "Let the same mind be in you that was in him." Let it be. How can we let it be? By letting go. This whole lesson teaches letting go the old working self. Jesus Christ bore our striving self once, mind and body, and as holding on to ourself is a great task which never amounts to anything, and makes us very tired, we now let go ourself and its struggles, and let what will be take its own course, since its whole destiny is safe in the keeping of that mighty character.

Think away, ye thinkers, training your subconscious mind with careful suggestions. Last Sunday's lesson declared that now, just at your flagging time, the un-thought of is near. Exercise still ye working missionaries. The actual fulfillment is near. But that which is near and does the wonderful things does not ask your efforts of mind or body. It asks that you let go the reins held so hard on yourself and let be what is; let now be visible what already has taken place. This is denial divine.

Inter-Ocean Newspaper, March 1, 1896

LESSON X

"Me, Imperturbed"

Luke 10:25-37

Today's lesson is farewell to Galilee, and salutation to the Perean campaign. Perea means "beyond." So when the Perean ministry began, it was eminently fitting that the first discussion should be upon eternal life. (See Luke 10:25-37).

This "eternal life" of which they are speaking in this section is something beyond continuance of conscious mind. It. is full sight of Self powers and ability to use them. Lawyers are always practicing on their self powers and using them to the height of their abilities, so it was meet that a lawyer should ask the Wisdom Man who was preaching in a private house where he was stopping, about how to get hold of his birthright.

Jesus of Nazareth then spoke in such a way that those who were receiving his teachings on the ideal, suggestion, or mind to mind plane, should be enlightened beyond their usual state; those who are receiving them on the ministry of abstract, doctrine plane should be helped beyond their usual state, and those who were in unison with His own inmost understanding should be solidified to His substance beyond what they had been.

Those who were receiving His ministry as conscious suggestions for subconscious demonstrations, took Him to mean that they must keep up the written formula of verse 27 till they felt full of love as a result of self treatment. Paul was working on this plane almost all the time, "Hold fast the form of sound words," he said to Timothy. This lawyer had probably practiced talking to himself just as he was going to sleep every night as the best time to train his subconscious mind and make him smart and rich.

The present order of metaphysicians who talk to themselves just as they are falling into a doze at night are but repeating the Oriental practices of far-away ages. "I will meditate on Thee in the night-watches," said David.

That is now described as the susceptible time of mind. It is then that it is most able to carry out into visible affairs what is told it as already having taken place. It is the practice of affirmation "Affirm constantly," said Paul.

Those who were receiving. the doctrines of Jesus as abstract propositions which would operate through the airs and influence other people, understood Him to say that concentration on the Lord's Presence here forever would kindle the whole soul, strength, heart, mind, and make them soft and subtle with influential ethers. (Verse 27)

Mind Is Eternal And Changeless

The present order of metaphysicians who are practicing various forms of concentrated attention on the Lord's Presence here among us forever expecting; this concentration to work mighty miracles on themselves and others, are but reviving the ancient attempts to reconstruct the universe by knowing high doctrines. It is the ministry of high doctrines to permeate the hearts of men and rocks when somebody knows them. This is a second order of metaphysical procedure.

Those who were in unison with the Jesus Christ understanding, knew that He meant that their Mind was eternal, and changeless One, as in the beginning, now and forevermore; that this Mind was soul eternal and changeless; that this soul was heart eternal and changeless, that this heart was strength eternal and changeless; that eternal, changeless heart, strength is Life changeless and indestructible. They knew that He meant that this was their substance and they had no other. They knew that He meant only one substance when He spoke of love. Their neighbors were that substance, as they themselves were that substance.

They knew that He did not mean that we love another person as another form, or a God separate from ourselves, by the words "Love the Lord thy God and thy neighbor as thyself;" but that being indissolubly cemented everywhere, there is no difference anywhere. This being the true state of affairs, nobody ever does anything by his neighbor only what he is doing to himself, and knowing his own substance everywhere he has nothing to deal with any time only his own Self.

These last listeners felt their bodies and minds solidifying into their normal state by His words. They saw themselves in the normal. No change ever takes place in the normal. The normal is the Jesus Christ body changeless and endless. The mind of Jesus Christ is the body normal. It is never perturbed. It is never angry, disappointed, or unhappy. Nothing moves it. The normal spreads its soul quality through heaven and earth, and stars and skies, as it was 'In the beginning, is now and ever shall be."

Mind, soul, strength, heart, life — these are all names of the one endless cemented substance.

This normal is everybody's present state, future state. These people did not understand that Jesus was giving them a treatment to get normal, but they knew that their normal was what they had always been. They saw it. They felt it.

Each Wonders What The Other Means

Both the other two classes of listeners took it that he was giving them a treatment to get them into some state they wanted to get into. The lawyer understood that every person was his own idea performing around. He wanted to know how to make all persons better. He wanted to know how he could change his ideas. Some of the people who represented his ideas were those who believed that if one man could keep up a set of abstract propositions without regard to whether any particular person was treated by them or not, eventually all people would be changed.

All of these classes of listeners come to hear the spiritual teachings of this nineteenth century, and each class wonders what the other is talking about when he hears them talking on the Science of Spirit.

The man who stands up in his pulpit and talks about the conquering power within himself has played the priest of Verse 31, if his audience goes home and feels that it can conquer the hurting speeches of the family by self treatment. He is playing the Levite of Verse 32, if a man goes home and makes up his mind he can get along without his family if they want to be so hateful. He is playing the Samaritan of Verse 33, if he makes a single man go home and see that the ugliest and grossest member of his household is so beautiful and so inspired that every movement and every tone reminds him of Paradise.

The neighbor state is when the neighbor reminds us of the wonderful normal that has always been our state and their state. The recognition of the changeless in other people is compassion. It carries with it food, clothes, shelter, health. Nobody ever felt it without the creatures he felt it for were instantly restored. It took Daniel three and one half years to have compassion on Nebuchadnezzar. He saw him as a tyrant whom he must pray about. This is priestly. It never put anybody into his own self-recognition yet, and it never will. Then he saw Nebuchadnezzar as a well-punished man of sin. This caused him to pray for himself, lest he get into as great a slum of law. There was no compassion for himself or for Nebuchadnezzar either, in this mind. So the King and Daniel both ate their bread in foolishness. Finally Daniel saw the changeless, unperturbed normal in both the King and himself, and this was compassion. The King felt the brightness of his original judgment immediately restored unto him and his counselors and lords sought him as a sane man.

Preached Compassion Not Sympathy

Jesus Christ preached compassion, not sympathy. Let us notice this fact. The recognition of the changeless normal state in all people is compassion on them. Everything that hides the normal flees, at once before this "neighbor" sight. Poverty scampers to give the normal state a good show. David prayed to see the normal of himself. "Give me neither poverty nor riches," he said. Hunger and nakedness, languor and ignorance fall down because the normal is not willing for them to hide it, and when a man sees the normal anywhere, either in himself or others, the abnormal disappears. The normal state of man is never deceived. It is the Jesus Christ state. He is not ever caught saying that the other teachers of methods for finding the unperturbed balance are all wrong, impractical and inferior. He knows that they are all right. Their methods for sighting the Imperturbable Me, the Imperturbable You, the Imperturbable Them, are all good; one is about as capable as another. He sees it already. That is all. He has no system for getting anywhere. He is already there. He has no system of reciting Scripture verses to keep him back to his native estate. He already knows it — this self-recognition gives him plain sight of his human brethren; the goats and spiders also, as one cemented stuff called by many names, but always the same. To see our own kind anywhere has always been called love.

It is a perfection of vision. This is power. This is ability. This is Paradise. Jesus called it Samaritanism. He called it compassion. He called it eternal life. The mother is praised because she is of a class of phenomena, always discovering the indissoluble cement. The wife is praised for her eternal fidelity, when it is only that she is steadily seeing her own substance. The discovery of our own substance is "neighboring."

One is never afraid of a lion when he sees his own kind of eternal changeless substance in the beast. So the lion never eats that neighbor whether he is white or black of skin.

Jesus says in this lesson that it is the effort of men to see their own satisfied normal that makes them savage. Even Christian ministers practice running their virtues up and their co-laborers down. This is struggle of one sort to get a glimpse of their own normal estate. The man in this lesson did not try to see himself or his neighbors. So the "neighbors" tore him to pieces. Then some of them felt that their satisfied state was somewhere else. So they hurried and studied and recited Scripture.

It was no damage to them to hurry past the non-committal man in their road. They would soon find somebody or something that would look like their own substance. It was no credit to the Samaritan to do so much for the wounded man. He had found some of his own substance right then and there. How could he help nourishing it?

The wounded man is the one to imitate, if we want to imitate anybody mentioned in this lesson. He let everybody have his own way with him. At first he was a mere rag of misery because some people he met thought he could lead them back to their own satisfied native state. Secondly, he was weak and still because some people were so busy reciting Scripture verses that they could not see that his substance and theirs was one substance. Thirdly, just because he did not try and struggle, but let things act as they would with him, there came along his own substance into sight.

Whenever Jesus of Nazareth talked he moved his tongue for all time. "My words shall not pass away." You may urge your Sunday-School class to go and carry bouquets to hospital beds, likewise arnica and pills, saying that this is Samaritanism.

This is Christian practice. But very soon the hospital patients will see that they are only acting under mechanical orders, "patronizing them."

But Jesus Christ meant further than that, He meant that to see the cemented substance filling heaven and earth, the ground and our .bodies, is to arise in our native compassionateness and have enough and to spare everywhere and always. The motto of this lesson is, "Me, Imperturbed."

For no matter what transpires in our existence, we need not get mixed up in it, which is sympathy with it — but are to keep on taking what faith sends along undisturbed, because first, rendings; second, neglect; third, comfortings, is the unvarying history of one who lays his fate on the bosom of this universe and lets come what will. .

The universe is kind as a mother. Put down the struggle to find kindness. "Vis Medicattix Naturae." (The healing power of nature) The universe has a wonderful healing sweetness in her cemented unity. See how the tree, heals when it is cut. See how Jesus rises when He is buried. See how the man in this chapter rose up

sane and happy when fate had done her worst. What God hath cemented is unbreakable.

Inter-Ocean Newspaper, March 8, 1896

LESSON XI

Jesus is Close to Men

Lord's Prayer

Luke 11:1-13

This lesson asks us to contemplate the principle, of translation and transubstantiation. It shows how invisible and moveless substances are convertible into visible and fluctuating objects. Thales asked: "What is that invariable existence of which these, the visible, and the variable states?" And this Bible Lesson answers his question.

This lesson tells that all people are performing on the boards of human existence, with more or less intelligent admission that they are trying to get something that is out of sight to show itself plainly to them.

One says he is cudgeling his senses like a Brahmin, starving himself like a Schlatter, or preaching high doctrine like a Zoroastrian to find that invariable and moveless stuff out of which he was made. Why does he want to find it? That he may show a power like it, of course.

There is a purpose in all religious operations, whether carried on by a fakir or a Christian orator. This lesson throws the whole mass of their effort into one word, namely, prayer.

This lesson repeats the high information given in the March 1st chapter that the Jesus Christ healing of the world is yet to be taught. The best healing of bodily or mental derangements yet taught has been only a hypnotic practice. If a man speaks with his silent mind to his neighbor and the neighbor obeys him even to the point of getting well of a lameness, he has hypnotized his neighbor. The doctrine of Jesus was: "See thou tell no man." All that translates itself from the wonderful stuff which moves not should be done by its own will and nature and not by the will of the man who heals.

The perfect way of praying, said the matchless man of Nazareth, is to address all speech, all thought, all vision, all touch, to the Father. Father means starting point.

<u>Bodies and Minds are but Taverns</u>

Then there will be many and mighty things transpire. Jesus teaches that this Father is in no way interested in our breakfast or our clothes and yet by addressing Him persistently He transubstantiates himself into breakfasts and clothes or anything else He is importuned to turn into.

This lesson teaches that the Father, who keeps Himself so steadily within us is not in our minds, neither is He in our bodies. Both body and mind are taverns, or inns, where the Father is never found.

There was one Bible lesson many Sundays ago which, explained positively that there was no room for Him in the inn nineteen hundred years ago, and there is no room there for Him now. So it was not in mind where Jesus was looking when, as last Sunday's lesson showed, He was praying to the Father within Himself. It was not in body, where Jesus was looking while alone praying to Himself.

It was the high throne which, like a point of fire, forever burning everywhere, forever; followed Him, as it follows each of us. And out of its moveless following flame he manufactured whatever He mentioned. He did not have to speak to a withered hand in order to heal it. He did not have to think toward it in order to heal it. His sight and thought were directed toward. His own starting point, or Father, and that Father acted according to His own nature, making the watching vision of Jesus a highway to glide over as clear window-glass makes a highway for sunshine to stream through.

"What I say unto you, I say unto all — watch," said Jesus. He did not mean, "Watch death, fire, wrath."

Pythagoras had heard of the point that all men came from and had heard that it was within himself. But he could not find it, he went from temple to temple in Egypt, trying to find a teacher who could show him where to look for it and how to look at it. He never found that teacher.

These lessons are very plain on that direction. They show that whatever a man mentions while watching that Father of himself is sure to happen unto him.

Name of Starting Point Unspeakable

This lesson fitly follows last Sunday's, which explained that each man who discovers his own substance that he came forth from soon discovers it everywhere he looks.

Today the disciples are eager to know how to pray to their own head center, that they too, like Jesus, may translate from the invisible into the visible.

Then Jesus succinctly declares that the same point of glory set them going which set himself going. “Our Father,” He said, Luke 9:1-13. He briefly announces that the name of the starting point is unspeakable by tongue or thought. “Hallowed be Thy Name,” He said. He, with a short sentence, covers all the ground of all men's general wishes about what they want of the Father. They want His kind of power through them, in them, to work on their world for them, everywhere. “Thy Kingdom Come, Thy Will Be Done. As In Heaven, So In Earth,” He said.

Remember that He was looking upward and backward exactly like Schlatter; while He is receiving what He calls healing streams from the Father, and exactly as Beethoven is looking while conceiving musical strains.

He is not looking at the skies. For the Father is not in that inn. He is not looking at the heart in his bosom, for the Father is not in that inn. There is a practice of repeating high reasonings to the far-stretching spirit that spreads itself, telling it of its glory and power. This is one way of making the glory and power manifest. It is the act of telling abroad what is true for the purpose of seeing its works where we have not yet seen them.

It is translating the invisible, into the visible. But Jesus seems to have kept all His addresses to the Most High as addresses to Himself. "I and the Father are one." "He that hath seen Me hath seen the Father." Then after such addresses to Himself He found His own substance everywhere and thus all things showed Him His own Father and quality, or nothing at all. It is daily reviving to see daily the wonderful Father or invariable substance which transubstantiates itself into new protections and new feelings. So Jesus prayed on; "Give us day by day our daily bread."

Ignorance of Evil is Sweet Bread

It is easy to translate by talk, high sounding oratory, the word bread into the realm of thoughts, by saying bread means sustaining thoughts. But Jesus meant more than sustaining thoughts. He meant that our substance, invariable and moveless, should be so watched by us and so addressed by us that its transit over our vision should turn it into whatever we should like for the day.

If bread and fruit and milk should be needed they should be forthcoming day by day. If intelligent thoughts should be needed they should be forthcoming day by day. If power or strength or beauty or life should be needed, they also should be forthcoming day by day. If total ignorance should be needed it also should be forthcoming. For ignorance of evil is bread of a sort sweet to eat. "Deliver us from evil," Said Jesus.

Forgiveness is the whole theme of Jesus in a sentence. That is, giving for. We throw toward the Father our silly concepts. The Father quality dissolves them and gives for them wisdom. It is always the opposite of what we send toward the Father on the throne where we came from that we feel coming over the lines. We all have beliefs in our own mistakes in life. We offer up these mistakes and for them is given readjustment of affairs. We say to the Father, the throne one from whom we were born, that we have wasted or lost our opportunities. The Father gives for that confession the golden glory of restoration of opportunities.

When a man calls us stingy or sinful or chimerical (no existence except in thought), or impractical and we know better, and we steadfastly know better, whose idea wins, do you think? Truly it is the idea on the good and wise, and capable side. And His idea dissolves in our own steady knowledge of the good fact. This is forgiveness.

So the Father is so different from our ideas, our beliefs that His hot fire of difference melts down our acknowledgments.

This is confession of sins. This is dissolving thereof. That wonderful One giving down of His substance freely, is giving for. It is forgiveness. It is transubstantiation. The Father quality on the throne of our own being is equal to anything. There was a blind man who looked upward toward the Father and said pitifully: "I am blind." Instantly that idea of his was dissolved. The natural gift of the Father came suddenly down. His sight came. That was forgiveness. He told the Father just what he thought was true of himself. That Father is the unconvinceable one.

Most Marvelous of Themes

If we do not hold steadfastly to our great and noble opinion of ourself when our fellow travelers are speaking ill of us, we shall never dissolve their opinion.

The Father is steadfast, immovable, unconvinceable. This is His giving for ability. He never agrees with us, no matter what we tell Him. Thus we are forgiven more and more. No theme so marvelous as that of forgiveness.

The Father the divine spark of our own life, knows nothing of our strange notions; knows nothing of our wants, lacks, needs. His opposite to them is His substance. Turning toward Him is offering our empty cups. Steadfastly holding our ideas of emptiness toward the all-supplying substance, the unlikeness of our petition to the facts of the case is all melted. The daisy draws down her substance from the sun. This is transubstantiation. The sun draws up her empty cup. So, forever and forever, draweth the "Sun of righteousness with healing in His wings — our faces toward His filling glory." "I draw them with the bands of love and they knew not that I heard them."

The ignorance of the divine throne-place of our being concerning our wants is because of its oppositeness to wants. Jesus Christ is willing to liken the Father to an un-sympathizing friend, as in verse 7, if He can, by so doing, teach us to hold up our private opinions of ourselves and our affairs before the face of the Father till His melting sunshine has forgiven them.

Is Not a Son an Idea

"I beheld His countenance as the sun shining in His strength," said John, who loved the theme of this lesson better than any other. Verse 11 shows how certainly forgiveness of poverty is translation from the invariable substance to the daily needs.

The world of opposite with its varying states has the offer of attending to the moveless sun of the everywhere present Father and being forgiven for its oppositeness. That is, given for. Its prayer should be: "Forgive me for existence, past, present, and future; forgive me for existence." Let it hold up its hard belief that it is a substance, when it is only a want, a desire, an emptiness, till its hard belief is melted and the emptiness is God. Thus shall the prophecy come true that "The earth shall be filled with the knowledge of the Lord as the waters fill the sea."

The most satisfying request to make to the Father is that we be forgiven for our opinions, first that we exist, second that we lack, third that we get off the right track, fourth that we are hurt. Forgiveness. Giving for. It is not a question of wickedness, but of opinions, beliefs. Wheresoever we behold the face of the Father that Father's face is the melting sunshine and the readjusting substance.

No other kind of interpretation of this section can fit this age. Jesus Himself said He had offered up His son of perdition till that eon was all lost. "Of all that Thou gavest me I have lost not one save the son of perdition."

Is not a son an idea? His idea of perdition was melted, and down through the free highway of His being came, and still comes, bread, daily bread, sweet joy, daily. New and wondrous life daily.

The forgiveness principle is the transubstantiation principle. At its final movement, it is heaven coming swiftly through all the earth as health steals swiftly through all the life when we are forgiven for sickness. Individually it is the divine I AM of each man manifesting in face, actions, speech, power, glory.

Inter-Ocean Newspaper March 15, 1896

Lesson XII

"Be Not Drunk With Wine."

Luke 12:37-46

"Money is not exactly what mountain promontories over public roads were in old times. The barons fought for them fairly. The strongest and cunningest got them; then fortified them, and made every one who passed below pay toll. Well, capital now is exactly what crags were then. Men fight fairly (we will at least grant so much, though it is more than we ought) for money; but once having got it, the fortified millionaire can make everybody who passes below pay toll to his million, and build another tower on his money castle. And I can tell you the poor vagrants by the roadside suffer now quite as much from the bag-barons as ever they did from the crag-barons. Bags and crags have just the same result on rags." — Ruskin.

Napoleon said; "When conscience gets rein, my reign ceases."

It was Jesus Christ who had a way of understanding things that made him independent of crags, bags, wine and conscience. He knew that to watch any of these things, even without any special interest in them, would finally set them to lording it over us.

Today's lesson is about lords many and gods many, but only one fact in this universe. The lesson makes it plain that the lords many and gods many, of men, are all delusions.

Jesus Christ often called the changeless One by the name of Lord, but this was only when illustrating his meaning by an example of cause arid effect, as this chapter of Luke 12:27-48. He loved better, however, the titles, "I", "Father", My Name". By this chapter he shows that these last terms have the effect of landing each one who uses them back onto his own position; his own vantage ground; standing place. They turn him around. They cause him to watch in another direction from that in which the philosophers and preachers are urging us to look. They keep a man from fighting for temperance, freedom, life, health, honor, home, or good in any form.

They make light of so-called glorious principles of our forefathers. How absurd, under the Lord of this lesson it would be to

"Strike! for our altars and our fires!

Strike for the green graves of our sires,

God, and our native land."

For the Lord of this lesson is capable of taking care of himself and us, too. And the marvel of it is that what happens is always the very good we were taught to strike and fight for.

Contagion From The Fightless God

The International Bible lesson book says: "God curse the saloon business." But Jesus of Nazareth said that the only thing he let go of was his idea that there was something to hate, curse, stamp on. (See last Sunday's lesson.) He taught that there is a contagion from the fightless God which is much more efficient then fighting for God. This contagion takes care of our altars and our fires, our native land, and everything else.

Moody , the revivalist, is chronicled in a certain book, to have said he would rather have his son's eyes dug out than to have him go down to his grave without Christ.

St. Jerome said: "Trample on thy father, trample on thy mother, and fly to the Lord, who calleth thee."

They were fighting for Christ. But Christ does not need fighting for, either by eloquent oratory or Krupp guns. He is quite capable of taking care of himself, and of a world full besides.

They are striking for the good. But the good does not need being struck for. This lesson gives away the whole principle of achievement. Whoever fights for the good is such a believer in the bad that the bad is a regular lord over him. So much so that some very dreadful things finally happen unto him.

Verses 46 and 47 call these things that happen to pious fighters on the side of the good "stripes" and "cuttings."

This lesson shows that the secret of the power of Jesus of Nazareth consisted in his being on a base out of the touch of good and bad. But from this position he is able to tell about the movements of good, and the movements of bad; the sweepways of light and the deep ways of darkness. Marat said he was inspired of God. Read up what he did and see that he represents how those who fight for good have no vantage ground from which to observe anything. All they can do is to load and fire in the ranks. If any man has a bad temper he can never conquer it on the Marat plan so but that it shows out in some form. But if he touch the position of this lesson he has nothing to conquer and nothing to suffer. The temper is nowhere, not even in a suppressed disease.

Stepping Back to the First Estate

The position taken according to this section of Luke, beginning with thirty-seventh verse, makes a new floor to walk on and a new air to breathe. Yet not new. They are the highway and oxygen native to us since before the foundations of the world.

This lesson gives us the way of stepping back to our first estate. It is by not stepping at all. By stopping our steps. Take notice, the actual Lord "cometh," "girdeth himself," "cometh forth and serveth." It is the nature of the Actual to accomplish the whole business in hand.

If any one does not believe this, but still he takes the position mentioned in this chapter, the accomplishing movements will go on just the same. Blessed be the name so hallowed no man can speak it, this Lord of Jesus Christ asks none of our faith to prod him on or up with, but achieves by his own potentiality. (Verse 37)

The figure of speech used to mark us with in this Luke, twelfth chapter, is "servants." The position we as men and women take with the mind and body of us toward our own head center is that of receiving according to its giving.

The head center of us never hurts us and never honors us. But no weapon against us can prosper; no friends or admirers can set us up. This Lord cementeth us to independence and nothing can part us from independent bread and independent house.

"He girdeth himself" by protecting us, for we are his own substance.

Twice in the scriptures is the idea of "making us to sit down to our table" made very strong.

Once by David and once by Jesus. The divine head center of us all, just above, just behind, everywhere we go, has a way of making us do things. Yet it is always ourselves doing them. Jesus of Nazareth set out to let his own head center of divinity run his affairs, manage his body, speak for him, think for him. "The words that I speak unto you, it is not I that speak but the Father that dwelleth in me, he doeth the works."

Thus he had something for his Lord, which kept him from fighting, and yet made him victorious.

"My kingdom is not of this world; if it were, then would my servants fight."

His servants were his thoughts, his hands, his will. His achievements would have ranked with Alexander's, Pompey's, Napoleon's, Caesar's, had he used his servants as his school teachers and ministers said was wise and brave.

Jesus in the Guise of a Soldier

He would have fought like Grant, McClellan, and Lincoln for the liberty of the blacks if he had had the Beecher and Sumner to teach him how to perform. But he had the fightless, moveless, changeless One for his teacher. As a good, soldier never takes his eye off his officer, so Jesus undertook to keep his eye forever on his head center. So he got contagion from on high. So he got the knack of doing everything by stopping his actions and of having everything by receiving what came and holding on to nothing. This was contagion from on high. This was his Lord's way.

Today's lesson illustrates the marvelous theme of contagion. Ruskin got his contagion from watching men at their fights. It had a strange effect on his head. He did not dissolve any of the abuses he kept his eyes on. They lorded it over him. The temperance people keep their eyes sharp on the movements of alcohol and opium. So these things have a queer effect upon them.

They never accomplish anything. They make no headway at all. This is a kind of drunken paralysis. It is wine to their minds to read about the crimes of the intoxicated. It is wine to their thoughts to orate with eloquent tongues about stupid sots. This wine to the mind and thought is very red, with a seeming nobility. But, as this lesson declares, they are parted asunder from what they want to accomplish, for when mental wine gets to seething, it is as drowsing to achievement as red grape wine. Our wine is what we are interested in. When it seems like a great cause for us to scream for, work for, fight for, then it is red.

"Look not upon the wine when it is red." No; for the thing we are looking at gets to lording it over us, whether it be opium or iniquity.

Jesus here calls it "watching." He said he was watching the uncontagioned One, that he should show in his own body that his contagion was from on high, where the enlivener, the provider, the protector, the empowerer abides.

"When people tell us they catch the disease of the people their thoughts go out upon, that is evidence where they are watching. They had better stop letting their thoughts go anywhere. They had better see what the mighty One on high is capable of doing without asking them to think, without asking them to speak, without asking them to move hand or foot.

Capital and Paper Question

"The Lord shall fight for you and you shall hold your peace."

They will find there is a Lord worth watching. This lesson gives the only solution to the capital and pauper question there can possibly be. Not a millionaire has been touched to do a single practical thing for the masses whose money he has dragged away by being stronger and shrewder than they, by any man's eloquence as Ruskin's or Tillman's, or Dixon's. Instead, the hardness of the millionaire gives the Ruskin bang at the end. For whatsoever a man watch, does indeed, get to lording it over him.

Now, Jesus of Nazareth touches in verse 45 on the chief reason why even the noble hearted reformers do not keep their attention fixed on the Mighty One that stirreth not. It is because he seems so slow. They feel as if they were wiser than to be so inactive. So they flourish and talk and write and fight. If they got ahead any by these struggles it would count as wisdom to kill and shout. But let it be distinctly understood that all freedom, health, wisdom, peace, now experienced by mankind, has been brought down over the lines by the silent watches of the fightless, moveless God, and not by swords or tongues.

In verse 46 Jesus declares that these reformers who are watching cronies and money-barons will be utterly astonished that they shall themselves suffer so much and never see anything they have fought for accomplished. This is being cut asunder from their wished-for results.

In verse 48 Jesus teaches that the times and season of the Most High One are early enough. He teaches that the results are full enough to satisfy the most greedy. Here he touches upon the greed for power which Napoleon had. Poor Napoleon. He caught sight of conscience and it whispered something about his doing the wrong way to get power. He was pricked by it, but he did not stop fighting to get his fill of power. This lesson says that no matter what the cause is, the fightless God is the one to watch. His bread of power is enough for the most greedy. His bread of wisdom is enough for the hungriest. His bread of satisfaction is enough for the most empty.

The dispensing benefactor must have arisen in our midst, here somewhere, for the committee to have chosen this theme for today.

For nothing is spoken from the mouth of the Jesus Christ man but what carries on its breath the substance of the all-accomplishing One upon whom his eyes wore fixed. Much has been committed to somebody, and they are now ready to dispense much. What are their names and where do they live?

Inter-Ocean Newspaper March 22, 1896

LESSON XIII

The Winds Of Living Light

Luke 12:8

Zoroaster discovered that four classes of people touch moments of inspiration with answers to prayer, namely, the afflicted, the seekers after truth, and the knowers of God.

Today's Bible lesson is about inspiration from the winds of living light that are forever blowing moveless elixirs everywhere. These Bible lessons all deal with the hitherto secret things concerning inspiration. These secret things have to be openly expressed in this age. They have been kept hidden from the foundations of the world till now. Many people are taking them up and shouting them from pulpits and exposing them through writings, all polished and decked with new forms of expression. But somewhere there must be diamonds in the rough, and they are the first handlings of the deep and mighty things of the everlasting One, as found in these interpretations.

There is something that is by Itself, and to it all things owe existence. It does not exist yet its influence is forever an inspiration to existence. To exist is to stand forth, to expose, to manifest. All matters, all mind, is existence, because it exposes itself. But nothing like the mighty One to which existence owes itself has ever been seen or touched or heard. Its influence is seen, felt, heard. This is inspiration.

The instant any man should see that One he would not exist; that is, he would not be seen, or heard, or touched. "No man can see my face and live."

The instant any man should see the mighty One, and disappear, he would himself become an Influence like It. If any man should keep his eye on the mighty One he would have a singular charm about him; an unexplainable authority, an influence and power wholly incommensurate with his external advantages.

He might be feeble of body, old of years, short of money, lacking in friendships, but he would win something everywhere, from man and fate, which other men are all eager after, you cannot win.

<u>How Success of a Day is Wrought Out</u>

Many a human being does unconsciously, or unwittingly, keep his eye toward the Mighty One, and there do follow him (or her) singular phenomena, or conditions. These people all have peculiar outward expressions of eyes. Take notice of them. Examine Paderewski's! Do they not look like the sensitive film upon which sounds are first pictured and then exhibited at 10 cents a song in the way stations or railroads?

Look at the eyes of the author of "Science and Health." They appear exactly the same. Are they bright and penetrating? No! Just the opposite. What are they doing? Catching things unlearnable. Things which cannot be taught — things which can only be caught. Now, when the eyes of the inner heart are purposely set for the unspeakable things of the changeless God, the works of such people live and live and live.

The stars dissolve and the pyramids fade, but their words and works are still gleaming with beauty and wonder.

Listen to David's psalms. Listen to the words of Jesus. Sit before a Raphael canvas. Though the grave should have covered your last friend, though the night should have closed on your years, all would be forgotten as their beams from the sweet fire of eternity are felt subtly stealing into your heart. It is very well to study rhetoric; it is very well to study human actions; but it is capability at catching what lies back of rhetoric, what is subtler than human actions, that makes what is done alive and enchanting.

This lesson explains that the success of a day is sometimes wrought out by becoming a sensitized film to the animus, or principal feeling of the age in which you live. That was the way Wellington got ahead of Napoleon. Some people explain that if this and that had not have happened Wellington would not have won the day. That is true. But those very things had to happen to act as weapons and aid-de-camp, for the execution of the feeling of the age caught for the moment in the sensitized plate of a Wellington.

We can all become sensitized plates to the things that we choose out of the flying feelings of this age. We need not take feelings. We may take ways and means. Be as noncommittal in the presence of something you would like to be or do, as Paderewski to the harmonies that are flying, and then act whatever way the first impulse leads. Be non-intelligent, non-committal even, with mind's best instructions for a certain period of time each day till all your activities, when next you move, make haste to carry out what you have caught.

"With you, make sure,
The stars will strive to
do your will.

Wishes of Men Shall Be Carried Out

The sun shall stand still on Gibeon, and the moon in the valley of Askelon, to carry out your wishes. So it is with a musician. His practice on the instrument is his first impulse. So it is with the author. His eagerness to write is his first activity. And, as sure as the stars sweep on in fearless certainty, arriving on time at their un-computed destinations, so sure is what you do a power in your day.

This lesson also tells of being a power forever, like Jesus and David and John. This is by being sensitized throughout all the extremities of existence, to the divine glory, the ceaseless majesty, that were our own before ever the most ancient of the stars were set swinging, but ever music or power or love was set going. There is, to be sure, nothing but the golden text to tell this meaning by, but this golden text swells and rolls and dies away toward the horizons, coming again forward with diviner symphonies of this meaning as the mystic hymns of the Russian choirs swell and fall and linger and arise on the ears of their enchanted worshippers. Read it: "Whosoever shall confess me before men, him shall the Son of Man also confess before the angels of God." (Luke 12:8)

Take notice, "Confess me before men." Can we not see that Wellington was negative to let the animus of many nations of indignant men find its focus in him? So he confessed, or agreed with men, first, as their war inspirations influenced the airs. But Jesus Christ said: "Confess me before men." Never mind what are the present feelings, tastes, strong inclinations of men; find me first — "me". Moses was on the same theme — the “me”. "Thou shalt have no gods before me." Nothing shall be so good as to tempt man from his own "me".

Lack Of Knowledge Is Wisdom

Let the folded wings of existence be spread from the me at the head the throne of the everlasting, who hath no interest in battles or pianos. This is conferring the "me" first, before men.

Many people suppose that this text means that we ought to know all we can about the personal history of the Carpenter of Nazareth. But truly he spoke of himself only because he knew that he was alive with the "me" everywhere.

Whatever we are eager to confess, or agree with or be at one with let us know nothing in its presence. Then its knowledge is our knowledge.

Therefore, there is a wise axiom to speak before standing in the presence of that with which we would be charged. It is this: "The less I know the greater my wisdom." If Wellington had graven his reasonings on the face of the animus of the nations when it reached him in its perfection at Waterloo he would not have acted in the power of its might.

So, in the presence of the Mighty One, of whom Moses and David and Jesus spake, "Thou shalt not make unto thee any graven image."

Angels are the highest thoughts about God, the sweetest, purest, best thoughts that men have ever thought. The state of being non-intelligent, non-thinking, in the presence of the Me, is more speedy and more glorious for man than his best imaginations, though they be wonderful imaginings. "I will confess him that maketh me so marvelously first that he graveth no thought across my shining countenance, greater in wisdom and more like me than the most sublime conceptions of man by pen or mind." This is confessing him in precedence of angels.

The four classes of men named by Zoroaster may hereby find Him of whom Moses and the prophets did write. The afflicted may take their choice of what to be non-committal in the presence of, that its influence may steal through them and master the world for their sakes. They may wait for the glories and greeds of this age to take hold of them and twist their fortunes into shape for them as Jay Gould, or Marlborough, or Cleveland, or they may wait in non-committal state for the divine Me on the throne of their being to lift them out of and away from pain, sorrow, and misfortune. So may the poverty- stricken. So may the seekers after God. So may the knowers of God.

<u>The Secret of Point Is Exposed</u>

This lesson has its secret point now for this instant exposed. It is that knowers of God are those who grave the most artful images across the face of the changeless and everlasting Me, thereby best deceiving the world, for their knowledges are the angels that fly on pinions of beauty, hiding like gauzy clouds the countenance of the Sun shining in his strength.

The greatest musicians are those who know the least in the presence of the wandering symphonies speeding forever through the airs, so the mightiest exponents of the divine One of whose powers and promises the lessons of this past quarter have been telling, are those who know the least about him, who describe him least; in whose radiant presence they are willingly nothing, letting his influence be their influence, letting his glory be their glory, letting his ways be their ways. If Wellington and Hannibal and Caesar could cease from being anything but focuses of the war spirit of their ages, if Beethoven and Mozart could cease from being anything but film-prepared cylinders for the sounds of the harp, the piano, and lyre, shall there not be one in our age to cease from being anything but a focus for the rays of the Eternal and Mighty God?

The Inter Ocean Newspaper, March 29, 1896

Notes

Other Books by Emma Curtis Hopkins

- *Class Lessons of 1888 (WiseWoman Press)*
- *Bible Interpretations (WiseWoman Press)*
- *Esoteric Philosophy in Spiritual Science (WiseWoman Press)*
- *Genesis Series 1894 (WiseWoman Press)*
- *High Mysticism (WiseWoman Press)*
- *Self Treatments with Radiant I Am (WiseWoman Press)*
- *Gospel Series (WiseWoman Press)*
- *Judgment Series in Spiritual Science (WiseWoman Press)*
- *Drops of Gold (WiseWoman Press)*
- *Resume (WiseWoman Press)*
- *Scientific Christian Mental Practice (DeVorss)*

Books about Emma Curtis Hopkins and her teachings

- *Emma Curtis Hopkins, Forgotten Founder of New Thought – Gail Harley*
- *Unveiling Your Hidden Power: Emma Curtis Hopkins' Metaphysics for the 21st Century (also as a Workbook and as A Guide for Teachers) – Ruth L. Miller*
- *Power to Heal: Easy reading biography for all ages –Ruth Miller*

To find more of Emma's work, including some previously unpublished material, log on to:

www.highwatch.org

www.emmacurtishopkins.com

WISEWOMAN PRESS
Vancouver, WA 98665
800.603.3005
www.wisewomanpress.com

Books by Emma Curtis Hopkins

- *Resume*
- *The Gospel Series*
- *Class Lessons of 1888*
- *Self Treatments including Radiant I Am*
- *High Mysticism*
- *Genesis Series 1894*
- *Esoteric Philosophy in Spiritual Science*
- *Drops of Gold Journal*
- *Judgment Series*
- *Bible Interpretations: Series I, thru XXII*

Books by Ruth L. Miller

- *Unveiling Your Hidden Power: Emma Curtis Hopkins' Metaphysics for the 21st Century*
- *Coming into Freedom: Emily Cady's Lessons in Truth for the 21st Century*
- *150 Years of Healing: The Founders and Science of New Thought*
- *Power Beyond Magic: Ernest Holmes Biography*
- *Power to Heal: Emma Curtis Hopkins Biography*
- *The Power of Unity: Charles Fillmore Biography*
- *Power of Thought: Phineas P. Quimby Biography*
- *The Power of Insight: Thomas Troward Biography*
- *The Power of the Self: Ralph Waldo Emerson Biography*
- *Uncommon Prayer*
- *Spiritual Success*
- *Finding the Path*

Books by Ute Maria Cedilla

- *The Mysticism of Emma Curtis Hopkins*
- *Volume 1 Finding the Christ*
- *Volume 2 Ministry: Realizing The Christ One in All*

List of
Bible Interpretation Series
with dates from 1st to 22nd Series.

This list is for the 1st to the 22nd Series. Emma produced twenty eight Series of Bible Interpretations.

She followed the Bible Passages provided by the International Committee of Clerics who produced the Bible Quotations for each year's use in churches all over the world.

Emma used these for her column of Bible Interpretations in both the Christian Science Magazine, at her Seminary and in the Chicago Inter-Ocean Newspaper.

First Series

July 5 - September 27, 1891

Lesson 1	The Word Made Flesh *John 1:1-18*	July 5th
Lesson 2	Christ's First Disciples John 1:29-42	July 12th
Lesson 3	All Is Divine Order *John 2:1-11* (Christ's first Miracle)	July 19th
Lesson 4	Jesus Christ and Nicodemus *John 3:1-17*	July 26th
Lesson 5	Christ at Samaria *John 4:5-26* (Christ at Jacob's Well)	August 2nd
Lesson 6	Self-condemnation *John 5:17-30* (Christ's Authority)	August 9th
Lesson 7	Feeding the Starving *John 6:1-14* (The Five Thousand Fed)	August 16th
Lesson 8	The Bread of Life *John 6:26-40* (Christ the Bread of Life)	August 23rd
Lesson 9	The Chief Thought *John 7:31-34* (Christ at the Feast)	August 30th
Lesson 10	Continue the Work *John 8:31-47*	September 6th
Lesson 11	Inheritance of Sin *John 9:1-11, 35-38* (Christ and the Blind Man)	September 13th
Lesson 12	The Real Kingdom *John 10:1-16* (Christ the Good Shepherd)	September 20th
Lesson 13	In Retrospection Review	September 27th

Second Series

October 4 - December 27, 1891

Lesson 1	Mary and Martha *John 11:21-44*	October 4th
Lesson 2	Glory of Christ *John 12:20-36*	October 11th
Lesson 3	Good in Sacrifice *John 13:1-17*	October 18th
Lesson 4	Power of the Mind *John 14:13; 15-27*	October 25th
Lesson 5	Vines and Branches *John 15:1-16*	November 1st
Lesson 6	Your Idea of God *John 16:1-15*	November 8th
Lesson 7	Magic of His Name *John 17:1-19*	November 15th
Lesson 8	Jesus and Judas *John 18:1-13*	November 22nd
Lesson 9	Scourge of Tongues *John 19:1-16*	November 29th
Lesson 10	Simplicity of Faith *John 19:17-30*	December 6th
Lesson 11	Christ is All in All *John 20: 1-18*	December 13th
Lesson 12	Risen With Christ *John 21:1-14*	December 20th
Lesson 13	The Spirit is Able Review of Year	December 27th

Third Series

January 3 - March 27, 1892

Lesson 1	A Golden Promise *Isaiah 11:1-10*	January 3rd
Lesson 2	The Twelve Gates *Isaiah 26:1-10*	January 10th
Lesson 3	Who Are Drunkards *Isaiah 28:1-13*	January 17th
Lesson 4	Awake Thou That Sleepest *Isaiah 37:1-21*	January 24th
Lesson 5	The Healing Light *Isaiah 53:1-21*	January 31st
Lesson 6	True Ideal of God *Isaiah 55:1-13*	February 7th
Lesson 7	Heaven Around Us *Jeremiah 31 14-37*	February 14th
Lesson 8	But One Substance *Jeremiah 36:19-31*	February 21st
Lesson 9	Justice of Jehovah *Jeremiah 37:11-21*	February 28th
Lesson 10	God and Man Are One *Jeremiah 39:1-10*	March 6th
Lesson 11	Spiritual Ideas *Ezekiel 4:9, 36:25-38*	March 13th
Lesson 12	All Flesh is Grass *Isaiah 40:1-10*	March 20th
Lesson 13	The Old and New Contrasted Review	March 27th

Fourth Series

April 3 - June 26, 1892

Lesson 1	Realm of Thought *Psalm 1:1-6*	April 3rd
Lesson 2	The Power of Faith *Psalm 2:1- 12*	April 10th
Lesson 3	Let the Spirit Work *Psalm 19:1-14*	April 17th
Lesson 4	Christ is Dominion *Psalm 23:1-6*	April 24th
Lesson 5	External or Mystic *Psalm 51:1-13*	May 1st
Lesson 6	Value of Early Beliefs *Psalm 72: 1-9*	May 8th
Lesson 7	Truth Makes Free *Psalm 84:1- 12*	May 15th
Lesson 8	False Ideas of God *Psalm 103:1-22*	May 22nd
Lesson 9	But Men Must Work *Daniel 1:8-21*	May 29th
Lesson 10	Artificial Helps *Daniel 2:36-49*	June 5th
Lesson 11	Dwelling in Perfect Life *Daniel 3:13-25*	June 12th
Lesson 12	Which Streak Shall Rule *Daniel 6:16-28*	June 19th
Lesson 13	See Things as They Are Review of 12 Lessons	June 26th

Fifth Series

July 3 - September 18, 1892

Lesson 1	The Measure of a Master *Acts 1:1-12*	July 3rd
Lesson 2	Chief Ideas Rule People *Acts 2:1-12*	July 10th
Lesson 3	New Ideas About Healing *Acts 2:37-47*	July 17th
Lesson 4	Heaven a State of Mind *Acts 3:1-16*	July 24th
Lesson 5	About Mesmeric Powers *Acts 4:1-18*	July 31st
Lesson 6	Points in the Mosaic Law *Acts 4:19-31*	August 7th
Lesson 7	Napoleon's Ambition *Acts 5:1-11*	August 14th
Lesson 8	A River Within the Heart *Acts 5:25-41*	August 21st
Lesson 9	The Answering of Prayer Acts 7: 54-60 - Acts 8: 1-4	August 28th
Lesson 10	Words Spoken by the Mind *Acts 8:5-35*	September 4th
Lesson 11	Just What It Teaches Us *Acts 8:26-40*	September 11th
Lesson 12	The Healing Principle Review	September 18th

Sixth Series

September 25 - December 18, 1892

Lesson 1	The Science of Christ *1 Corinthians 11:23-34*	September 25th
Lesson 2	On the Healing of Saul *Acts 9:1-31*	October 2nd
Lesson 3	The Power of the Mind Explained *Acts 9:32-43*	October 9th
Lesson 4	Faith in Good to Come *Acts 10:1-20*	October 16th
Lesson 5	Emerson's Great Task *Acts10:30-48*	October 23rd
Lesson 6	The Teaching of Freedom *Acts 11:19-30*	October 30th
Lesson 7	Seek and Ye Shall Find *Acts 12:1-17*	November 6th
Lesson 8	The Ministry of the Holy Mother *Acts 13:1-13*	November 13th
Lesson 9	The Power of Lofty Ideas *Acts 13:26-43*	November 20th
Lesson 10	Sure Recipe for Old Age *Acts 13:44-52, 14:1-7*	November 27th
Lesson 11	The Healing Principle *Acts 14:8-22*	December 4th
Lesson 12	Washington's Vision *Acts 15:12-29*	December 11th
Lesson 13	Review of the Quarter	December 18th
	Partial Lesson Shepherds and the Star	December25th

Seventh Series

January 1 - March 31, 1893

Lesson 1	All is as Allah Wills *Ezra 1*	January 1st
Lesson 2	Zerubbabel's High Ideal *Ezra 2:8-13*	January 8th
Lesson 3	Divine Rays Of Power *Ezra 4*	January 15th
Lesson 4	Visions Of Zechariah *Zechariah 3*	January 22nd
Lesson 5	Spirit of the Land Zechariah 4:1-10	January 27th
Lesson 6	Dedicating the Temple Ezra 6:14-22	February 3rd
Lesson 7	Nehemiah's Prayer *Nehemiah 13*	February 12th
Lesson 8	Ancient Religions *Nehemiah 4*	February 19th
Lesson 9	Understanding is Strength Part 1 *Nehemiah 13*	February 26th
Lesson 10	Understanding is Strength Part 2 *Nehemiah 13*	March 3rd
Lesson 11	Way of the Spirit *Esther*	March 10th
Lesson 12	Speaking of Right Things Proverbs 23:15-23	March 17th
Lesson 13	Review	March 24th

Eighth Series

April 2 - June 25, 1893

Lesson 1	The Resurrection of Christ *Matthew 28:1-10*	April 2nd
Lesson 2	Universal Energy *Book of Job, Part 1*	April 9th
Lesson 3	Strength From Confidence *Book of Job, Part II*	April 16th
Lesson 4	The New Doctrine Brought Out *Book of Job, Part III*	April 23rd
Lesson 5	Wisdom's Warning *Proverbs 1:20-23*	April 30th
Lesson 6	The Law of Understanding *Proverbs 3*	May 7th
Lesson 7	Self-Esteem *Proverbs 12:1-15*	May 14th
Lesson 8	Physical vs. Spiritual Power *Proverbs 23:29-35*	May 21st
Lesson 9	Only One Power (information taken from Review)	May 28th
Lesson 10	Recognizing Our Spiritual Nature *Proverbs 31:10-31*	June 4th
Lesson 11	Intuition *Ezekiel 8:2-3, Ezekiel 9:3-6, 11*	June 11th
Lesson 12	The Power of Faith *Malachi*	June 18th
Lesson 13	Review of the 2nd Quarter *Proverbs 31:10-31*	June 25th

Ninth Series

July 2 - September 27, 1893

Lesson 1	Secret of all Power *Acts 16: 6-15*	July 2nd
Lesson 2	The Flame of Spiritual Verity *Acts 16:18*	July 9th
Lesson 3	Healing Energy Gifts *Acts 18:19-21*	July 16th
Lesson 4	Be Still My Soul *Acts 17:16-24*	July 23rd
Lesson 5	(Missing) Acts 18:1-11	July 30th
Lesson 6	Missing No Lesson *	August 6th
Lesson 7	The Comforter is the Holy Ghost *Acts 20*	August 13th
Lesson 8	Conscious of a Lofty Purpose *Acts 21*	August 20th
Lesson 9	Measure of Understanding *Acts 24:19-32*	August 27th
Lesson 10	The Angels of Paul *Acts 23:25-26*	September 3rd
Lesson 11	The Hope of Israel *Acts 28:20-31*	September 10th
Lesson 12	Joy in the Holy Ghost *Romans 14*	September 17th
Lesson 13	Review *Acts 26-19-32*	September 24th

Tenth Series

October 1 – December 24, 1893

Lesson 1	When the Truth is Known *Romans 1:1-19*	October 1st
Lesson 2	Justification, free grace, redemption *Romans 3:19-26*	October 8th.
Lesson 3	Justification by Faith *Romans 5:1-11* *Romans 12:1-15*	October 15th
Lesson 4	Christian Living *Romans 12:1*	October 22nd
Lesson 5	Comments on the Golden Text *I Corinthians 8:1-13*	October 29th
Lesson 6	Science of the Christ Principle *I Corinthians 12:1-26*	November 5th
Lesson 7	The Grace of Liberality *II Corinthians 8:1-12*	November 12th
Lesson 8	Imitation of Christ *Ephesians 4:20-32*	November 19th
Lesson 9	The Christian Home *Colossians 3:12-25*	November 26th
Lesson 10	*Grateful Obedience* *James 1:16-27*	December 3rd
Lesson 11	The Heavenly Inheritance *I Peter 1:1-12*	December 10th
Lesson 12	The Glorified Saviour *Revelation 1:9-20*	December 17th
Lesson 13	A Christmas Lesson Matthew 2:1-11	December 24th
Lesson 14	Review	December 31st

Eleventh Series

January 1 – March 25, 1894

Lesson 1	The First Adam *Genesis 1:26-31 & 2:1-3*	January 7th
Lesson 2	Adam's Sin and God's Grace *Genesis 3:1-15*	January 14th
Lesson 3	Cain and Abel *Genesis 4:3-13*	January 21st
Lesson 4	God's Covenant With Noah *Genesis 9:8-17*	January 28th
Lesson 5	Beginning of the Hebrew Nation *Genesis 12:1-9*	February 4th
Lesson 6	God's Covenant With Abram *Genesis 17:1-9*	February 11th
Lesson 7	God's Judgment of Sodom *Genesis 18:22-23*	February 18th
Lesson 8	Trial of Abraham's Faith *Genesis 22:1-13*	February 25th
Lesson 9	Selling the Birthright *Genesis 25:27-34*	March 4th
Lesson 10	Jacob at Bethel *Genesis 28:10-22*	March 11th
Lesson 11	Temperance *Proverbs 20:1-7*	March 18th
Lesson 12	Review and Easter *Mark 16:1-8*	March 25th

Twelfth Series

April 1 – June 24, 1894

Lesson 1	Jacob's Prevailing Prayer *Genesis 24:30, 32:9-12*	April 8th
Lesson 2	Discord in Jacob's Family *Genesis 37:1-11*	April 1st
Lesson 3	Joseph Sold into Egypt *Genesis 37:23-36*	April 15th
Lesson 4	Object Lesson in Genesis *Genesis 41:38-48*	April 22nd
Lesson 5	"With Thee is Fullness of Joy" *Genesis 45:1-15*	April 29th
Lesson 6	Change of Heart *Genesis 50:14-26*	May 6th
Lesson 7	Israel in Egypt *Exodus 1:1-14*	May 13th
Lesson 8	The Childhood of Moses *Exodus 2:1-10*	May 20th
Lesson 9	Moses Sent As A Deliverer *Exodus 3:10-20*	May 27th
Lesson 10	The Passover Instituted *Exodus 12:1-14*	June 3rd
Lesson 11	Passage of the Red Sea *Exodus 14:19-29*	June 10th
Lesson 12	The Woes of the Drunkard *Proverbs 23:29-35*	June 17th
Lesson 13	Review	June 24th

Thirteenth Series

July 1 – September 30, 1894

Lesson 1	The Birth of Jesus *Luke 2:1-16*	July 1st
Lesson 2	Presentation in the Temple *Luke 2:25-38*	July 8th
Lesson 3	Visit of the Wise Men *Matthew 1:2-12*	July 15th
Lesson 4	Flight Into Egypt *Mathew 2:13-23*	July 22nd
Lesson 5	The Youth of Jesus *Luke2:40-52*	July 29th
Lesson 6	The "All is God" Doctrine *Luke 2:40-52*	August 5th
Lesson 7	Missing	August 12th
Lesson 8	First Disciples of Jesus *John 1:36-49*	August 19th
Lesson 9	The First Miracle of Jesus *John 2:1-11*	August 26th
Lesson 10	Jesus Cleansing the Temple *John 2:13-25*	September 2nd
Lesson 11	Jesus and Nicodemus *John 3:1-16*	September 9th
Lesson 12	Jesus at Jacob's Well *John 4:9-26*	September 16th
Lesson 13	Daniel's Abstinence *Daniel 1:8-20*	September 23rd
Lesson 14	Review *John 2:13-25*	September 30th

Fourteenth Series

October 7 – December 30, 1894

Lesson 1	Jesus At Nazareth *Luke 4:16-30*	October 7th
Lesson 2	The Draught of Fishes *Luke 5:1-11*	October 14th
Lesson 3	The Sabbath in Capernaum *Mark 1:21-34*	October 21st
Lesson 4	The Paralytic Healed *Mark 2:1-12*	October 28th
Lesson 5	Reading of Sacred Books *Mark 2:23-38, Mark 3:1-5*	November 4th
Lesson 6	Spiritual Executiveness *Mark 3:6-19*	November 11th
Lesson 7	Twelve Powers Of The Soul *Luke 6:20-31*	November 18th
Lesson 8	Things Not Understood Attributed to Satan *Mark 3:22-35*	November 25th
Lesson 9	Independence of Mind *Luke 7:24-35*	December 2nd
Lesson 10	The Gift of Untaught Wisdom *Luke 8:4-15*	December 9th
Lesson 11	The Divine Eye Within *Matthew 5:5-16*	December 16th
Lesson 12	Unto Us a Child I s Born *Luke 7:24-35*	December 23rd
Lesson 13	Review *Isaiah 9:2-7*	December 30th

Fifteenth Series

January 6-March 31, 1895

Lesson 1	Missing *Mark 6:17-29*	January 6th
Lesson 2	The Prince Of The World *Mark 6:30-44*	January 13th
Lesson 3	The Golden Text *John 6:25-35*	January 20th
Lesson 4	The Golden Text *Matthew 16:13-25*	January 27th
Lesson 5	The Transfiguration Luke 9:28-36	February 3rd
Lesson 6	Christ And The Children *Matthew 18:1-14*	February 10th
Lesson 7	The Good Samaritan *Luke 10:25-37*	February 17th
Lesson 8	Christ And The Man Born Blind *John 9:1-11*	February 24th
Lesson 9	The Raising Of Lazarus *John 11:30-45*	March 3rd
Lesson 10	The Rich Young Ruler *Mark 10:17-27*	March 10th
Lesson 11	Zaccheus The Publican *Luke 1:10*	March 17th
Lesson 12	Purity Of Life Romans 13:8-14	March 24th
Lesson 13	Review	March 31st

Sixteenth Series

April 7-June 30, 1895

Lesson 1	The Triumphal Entry *Mark 11:1-11*	April 7th
Lesson 2	The Easter Lesson *Mark 12:1-12*	April 14th
Lesson 3	Watchfulness Mark 24:42-51	April 21st
Lesson 4	The Lord's Supper *Mark 14:12-26*	April 28th
Lesson 5	Jesus in Gethsemane Mark 15:42-52	May 5th
Lesson 6	The Jesus Christ Power *Mark 14:53-72*	May 12th
Lesson 7	Jesus Before Pilate *Mark 15:1-15*	May 19th
Lesson 8	The Day of the Crucifixion *Mark 15:22-37*	May 26th
Lesson 9	At the Tomb *Mark 16:1-8*	June 2nd
Lesson 10	The Road To Emmaus *Luke 24:13-32*	June 9th
Lesson 11	Fisher of Men *John 21:4-17*	June 16th
Lesson 12	Missing Luke 24:27-29	June 23rd
Lesson 13	Review	June 30th

Seventeenth Series

July 7 – September 29, 1895

Lesson 1	The Bread of Energy *Exodus 22:1-17*	July 7th
Lesson 2	Grandeur is Messiahship *Exodus 32:30-35*	July 14th
Lesson 3	Temperance *Leviticus 10:1-9*	July 21st
Lesson 4	The Alluring Heart of Man *Numbers 10:29-36*	July 28th
Lesson 5	As a Man Thinketh Numbers 13:17-23	August 4th
Lesson 6	Rock of Eternal Security *Numbers 31:4-9*	August 11th
Lesson 7	Something Behind *Deuteronomy 6:3-15*	August 18th
Lesson 8	What You See Is What You Get *Joshua 3:5-17*	August 25th
Lesson 9	Every Man To His Miracle *Joshua 6:8-20*	September 1st
Lesson 10	Every Man To His Harvest *Joshua 14:5-14*	September 8th
Lesson 11	Every Man To His Refuge *Joshua 20:1-9*	September 15th
Lesson 12	The Twelve Propositions Joshua 24:14-25	September 22nd
Lesson 13	Review I Kings 8:56	September 29th

Eighteenth Series

Oct 6 – December 29, 1895

Lesson 1	Missing	October 6th
Lesson 2	Gideon's Triumph *Judges 7:13-23*	October 13th
Lesson 3	The Divine Ego *Ruth 1:4-22*	October 20th
Lesson 4	All is Good *I Samuel 3:1-11*	October 27th
Lesson 5	If Thine Eye Be Single *I Samuel 7:5-12*	November 3rd
Lesson 6	Saul Chosen King *I Samuel 10:17-27*	November 10th
Lesson 7	Saul Rejected *I Samuel 15:10-23*	November 17th
Lesson 8	Temperance *Isaiah 5:11*	November 24th
Lesson 9	The Lord Looketh Upon the Heart *I Samuel 16:1-13*	December 1st
Lesson 10	Missing	December 8th
Lesson 11	The Third Influence *I Samuel 20:32-42*	December 15th
Lesson 12	The Doctrine of the Holy Land *Luke 2:8-9*	December 22nd
Lesson 13	Review	December 29th

Nineteenth Series

January 5 – March 29, 1896

Lesson 1	Missing	January 5th
Lesson 2	Missing	January 12th
Lesson 3	Lesson on Repentance *Luke 3:15-22*	January 19th
Lesson 4	"The Early Ministry of Jesus" *Luke 4:22*	January 26th
Lesson 5	Missing	February 2nd
Lesson 6	Missing	February 9th
Lesson 7	The Secret Note *Luke 6:41-49*	February 16th
Lesson 8	Answered Prayer *Luke 6:41-49*	February 23rd
Lesson 9	Letting Go The Old Self *Luke 9:18-27*	March 1st
Lesson 10	"Me, Imperturbed" *Luke 10:25-37*	March 8th
Lesson 11	Lord's Prayer *Luke 11:1-13*	March 15th
Lesson 12	Be Not Drunk With Wine *Luke 12:37-46*	March 22nd
Lesson 13	The Winds of Living Light *Luke 12:8*	March 29th

Emma Curtis Hopkins was absent on a voyage to Vera Cruz, Mexico to bring her ill son back to the USA. She left December 28, 1895 and returned February 6, 1896. This would account for missing lessons in this quarter. She may have mailed the two in January or they may have been written previously.

Twentieth Series

April 5 – June 28, 1896

Lesson 1	The Radiation of Light *Luke 13:22-30*	April 5
Lesson 2	The Great Supper *Luke 14:15-24*	April 12th
Lesson 3	The Radiation of Joy *Luke 15:11-24*	April 19th
Lesson 4	Out of the Range of Mind *Luke 16:19-31*	April 26th
Lesson 5	Going Toward Jerusalem *Luke 17:5-10*	May 3rd
Lesson 6	The Publican And The Pharisee *Luke 18:9-17*	May 10th
Lesson 7	The Last Great Week *Luke 19:11-27*	May 17th
Lesson 8	Unthinkable Divinity *Luke 20:9-19*	May 24th
Lesson 9	The Destruction Of Jerusalem Foretold *Luke 21:20-36*	May 31st
Lesson 10	Forgiveness for Hunger *Luke 22:22-47*	June 7th
Lesson 11	Forgiveness for the Unknown and the Undone *Luke 23:33-46*	June 14th
Lesson 12	The Risen Lord *Luke 24:36-53*	June 21st
Lesson 13	Review	June 28th

Twenty-First Series

July 5 – September 27, 1896

Lesson 1	The Lord Reigneth *II Samuel 2:1-11*	July 5th
Lesson 2	Adeptship *II Samuel 5:1-12*	July 12th
Lesson 3	The Ark *II Samuel 6:1-12*	July 19th
Lesson 4	Purpose of An Adept *II Samuel 7:4-16*	July 26th
Lesson 5	Individual Emancipatioin *II Samuel 9:1-13*	August 2nd
Lesson 6	The Almighty Friend *II Samuel 10:8-19*	August 9th
Lesson 7	Salvation Is Emancipation(missing) *Psalms 32:1-1*	August 16th
Lesson 8	Individual Emancipation *II Samuel 15:1-12*	August 23rd
Lesson 9	Absalom's Defeat And Death *II Samuel 16:9-17*	August 30th
Lesson 10	The Crown Of Effort *I Chronicles 22:6-16*	September 6th
Lesson 11	"Thy Gentleness Hath Made Me Great *II Samuel 22*	September 13th
Lesson 12	A Fool For Christ's Sake *Proverbs 16:7-33*	September 20th
Lesson 13	The Lord is a Strong Tower Proverbs 28:10	September 27th

September 27 of this quarter is a Review of the International Committee listing, not Emma's usual listing and review of the previous lessons in the quarter.

Twenty-Second Series

October 4 – December 27, 1896

Lesson 1	A Study in the Science of the Lightning *I Kings 1*	October 4th
Lesson 2	Solomon's Wise Choice *I Kings 3*	October 11th
Lesson 3	The Mysterious Adeptship Inherent In Us All *I Kings 4:25-34*	October 18th
Lesson 4	Missing	October 25th
Lesson 5	Building the Temple *I Kings 5:1-12*	November 1st
Lesson 6	The Dedication of the Temple *I Kings 8:54-63*	November 8th
Lesson 7	Converse With the Actual God *I Kings 9:1-9*	November 15th
Lesson 8	Rewards of Obedience *Proverbs 3:1-17*	November 22nd
Lesson 9	A Greater Than Solomon *I Kings 10:1*	November 29th
Lesson 10	Our Destined End or Way *I Kings 11:4-13, II Corinthians 10:12*	December 6th
Lesson 11	Solomon's Son *Proverbs 23:15-25*	December 13th
Lesson 12	Missing	December 20th
Lesson 13	Review *Ecclesiastes 12:13*	December 27th

Made in the USA
Columbia, SC
12 December 2017